SPIRIT ✢ SONG

A SEEKER'S GUIDE FOR LITURGY AND PRAYER

ASSEMBLY/GUITAR EDITION

OCP Publications

Publisher — John J. Limb
Editorial Director — Paulette McCoy
Executive Editor — Joanne Osborn
Editor — Thomas N. Tomaszek
Music Editor — Rick Modlin
Editing Assistance — Tony Barr, Ed Bolduc, Barbara Bridge, Scot Crandal, Carl Derfler, Geri Ethen, Robert Hawthorne, Sara Kramer, Kathy Orozco, Melissa Phong, Lori Modlin Rux, Eric Schumock, William Schuster, David Simmons, Robert Stoltz, Amanda Weller, Angela Westhoff-Johnson
Liturgical Consultant — James A. Wilde, Ph.D.
Music Engraving — Sharon Norton, Director; Christine Ambrose, Brian Healey, Jon Jonsson, Laura C. Kantor, Didi King, Shannon McNerney, Rick Modlin
Cover Art and Graphic Design — Judy Urben
Art Direction — Jean Germano

Edition No. 10804
ISBN 1-57992-007-1

PREFACE

Spirit & Song is a worship resource for parish youth ministries, Catholic schools, college campuses, and retreat centers that host youth and young adult groups. It is intended to be a user-friendly, comprehensive worship aid for celebrating Mass, sacramental celebrations, and prayer services with the younger generations. Due to the pastoral needs of many communities, *Spirit & Song* may also supplement other regularly-used hymnals and resources.

Spirit & Song has been designed to catechize youth about the form of liturgical prayer, and to help shape their worship along consistent liturgical norms. For example, a complete Order of Mass, featuring the *Mass of Glory* by Bob Hurd and Ken Canedo, has been included. In addition, there are three other complete Mass settings so those young musicians can learn seasonal rotation. A simple Guide to Preparing Mass and a Mass Preparation Form will assist those unfamiliar with the demands of ritual to plan a liturgy when parish or campus resources are not available to them. Similarly, orders of worship for Morning and Evening prayer and for Reconciliation have been included, so that young people may become more familiar with these rituals and use them regularly.

The liturgical music in *Spirit & Song* is arranged in sections by its primary ritual function: Songs for Gathering and Sending Forth, Psalms and Canticles, Mass Settings and other Ritual Music, and Communion Songs. We are particularly proud to present settings of all twenty-two common responsorial psalms, along with indexes to help liturgy teams use them seasonally. A final section of Songs for Prayer and Praise includes music that young people frequently sing in non-liturgical settings, though some songs also have liturgical applications. Many of these are well-known "standards" sung at youth conferences, retreats and other similar events. Licensing restrictions unfortunately prevented us from including several often-requested songs from other publishing companies.

Spirit & Song blends a variety of styles for ritual music, songs and hymnody. We have tried to balance sufficient amounts of well-known music with creative new songs that can lead all ages to vibrant worship. Many of the newer pieces are in contemporary styles very familiar to young people, but which may be less familiar to liturgical musicians. We acknowledge that the syncopated melodies and rhythms of contemporary styles may be challenging at first, but know that using these styles can also awaken the sung response of younger members of the assembly when used appropriately. We invite pastoral leaders to encourage and call forth the musical talents of youth and young adults to help find the creative balance of traditional and contemporary styles, and to help lead those newer musical styles in the full assembly.

The scope and size of *Spirit & Song* limited our ability to present a large variety of seasonal music. Consequently, we often chose a piece that had multiple applications over a more seasonally specific song. We hope the various indexes will be helpful in locating songs appropriate for the season, but recognize that other musical resources may be needed.

We faced similar challenges in choosing culturally diverse and bilingual music. Scope and size restricted the addition of more English-Spanish songs and more African-American hymnody. The *Mass of Glory*, composed in a Gospel/spiritual style, and *Misa del Mundo*, Jesse Manibusan's multilingual setting, are included partly for their cultural diversity. We must assume, however, that other resources will be needed to supplement *Spirit & Song* for culturally diverse circumstances.

All of the music in *Spirit & Song* is recorded and available in compact disc format, including some well-known songs that have been re-arranged or re-styled with fresh approaches. We hope these recordings will provide a reference for instrumentalists and choirs wanting to learn new material and new styles, and be a resource for personal prayer and group listening.

We wish to thank all who assisted in bringing *Spirit & Song* to life. We especially thank John Limb, OCP's publisher, for his vision, support, and willingness to pursue this resource for youth and young adults. We are truly grateful to Paulette McCoy, Joanne Osborn, and Randall DeBruyn for their leadership and guidance; James Wilde for his liturgical review; Steve Angrisano, Tom Booth, Ken Canedo, Jaime Cortez, Bob Hurd, Melanie Teska, and many youth, young adults and pastoral ministers for their advice during the music selection process; Ed Bolduc, Ken Canedo, Gerard Chiusano, Scot Crandal, Craig Kingsbury, Dominic MacAller, and Tim Smith for musical arrangements; Matt Navarre and David Simmons for technical assistance; Jean Germano and Judy Urben for artwork and cover design; and Joe Bellamy, Tom Booth, Jaime Cortez, Brian Green, Craig Kingsbury, Mike Moore, Jeff Roscoe, Timothy R. Smith, Don Turney, and Kevin Walsh for producing the recordings.

Finally, we thank seekers of all generations for the desire to lift their spirits in song. May the Holy Spirit continue to give us the courage and the voice to praise God for abundant mercy and love.

Thomas N. Tomaszek, Editor
Rick Modlin, Music Editor
The Assumption of the Virgin Mary into Heaven
August 15, 1999

CONTENTS

Mass Preparation Form

Day / Date / Time of Mass _____

Presider _____

Focus for Preparation_____

Prelude _____

Assembly Preparation _____

INTRODUCTORY RITES

Entrance Song _____

Rite of Sprinkling or Penitential Rite_____

Glory to God _____

Opening Prayer _____

LITURGY OF THE WORD

First Reading / Lector _____

Responsorial Psalm / Cantor _____

Second Reading / Lector _____

Gospel Acclamation _____

Gospel _____

Homily _____

Creed (Sundays and Feasts) _____

General Intercessions _____

LITURGY OF THE EUCHARIST

Preparation of Gifts & Table _____

Mass Setting: Holy, Memorial Acclamation, Amen _____

Lord's Prayer _____

Lamb of God _____

Eucharistic Ministers _____

Communion Song(s) _____

Song of Praise_____

Communion Prayer _____

CONCLUDING RITE

Final Blessing _____

Sending Forth _____

(This page may be reprinted as needed.)

THE ORDER OF MASS

Each time we gather for Mass, we are mindful of all the ways God walks with us in our daily faith journey. We gather, not just as individuals, but as the people of God, a community of believers giving glory and praise. Take some time before Mass begins, either through spirited singing, by greeting and welcoming those near you, or in private prayer, to open your mind and heart to the many ways God is present on this occasion.

INTRODUCTORY RITES

ENTRANCE SONG (GATHERING OR PROCESSIONAL)

Choose a song from the sections Gathering & Sending Songs (#97–148), or Psalms & Canticles (#53–96).

GREETING

In the name of the Father, and of the Son, and of the Holy Spirit.
Amen.

A   The grace of our Lord Jesus Christ and the love of God and the fellowship of the Holy Spirit be with you all.
And also with you.

B   The grace and peace of God our Father and the Lord Jesus Christ be with you.
Blessed be God, the Father of our Lord Jesus Christ.
or
And also with you.

C   The Lord be with you.
And also with you.

Additional Mass Settings and Ritual Music may be found in #20–52.

RITE OF BLESSING AND SPRINKLING HOLY WATER

On Sundays there may be a blessing and sprinkling of water to recall baptism. In that case the penitential rite and Kyrie are omitted. During the sprinkling, the following or another suitable hymn or song (or additional verses of the Entrance Song) may be sung.

1

Come to the River
Sprinkling Rite

Mass of Glory
Bob Hurd
Harmony by Craig Kingsbury

But in the Lord___ we shall a-rise.

VERSES

1. Washed in wa - ters of re - birth,___
2. Priest - ly peo - ple are___ we,___
3. Blest are those___ who___ thirst___
4. Let us walk___ in the light___
5. Those who sow___ in___ tears___

1. we have put on Christ Je - sus.___
2. sealed and sent by the Spir - it.___
3. for the reign of God's jus - tice.___
4. of God's ho - ly prom - ise.___
5. reap the har - vest re - joic - ing.___

PENITENTIAL RITE

This celebration of God's mercy takes one of the following forms:

A   I confess to almighty **God,**
and to you, my brothers and sisters,
that I have sinned through my own fault
in my thoughts and in my words,
in what I have done,
and in what I have failed to do;
and I ask blessed Mary, ever virgin,
all the angels and saints,
and you, my brothers and sisters,
to pray for me to the Lord our God.
May almighty God have mercy on us,
forgive us our sins, and bring us to everlasting life.
Amen.

B Lord, we have sinned against you:
Lord, have mercy.
Lord, have mercy.
Lord, show us your mercy and love.
And grant us your salvation.
May almighty God have mercy on us,
forgive us our sins,
and bring us to everlasting life.
Amen.

C
2

Lord, Have Mercy
Penitential Rite C

Mass of Glory
Bob Hurd
Harmony by Craig Kingsbury

*For shorter intro, begin here.

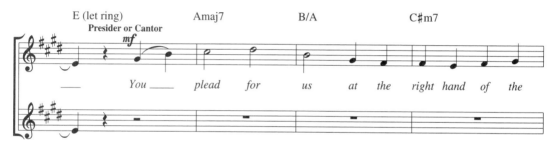

The invocations Lord, have mercy or Kyrie eleison follow, unless they have already been used in one of the forms above.

A   Lord, have mercy.
Lord, have mercy.
Christ, have mercy.
Christ, have mercy.
Lord, have mercy.
Lord, have mercy.

B
3

Kyrie Eleison

Mass of Glory
Bob Hurd
Arranged by Craig Kingsbury

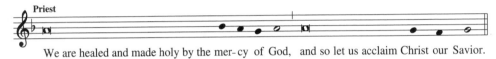

We are healed and made holy by the mer-cy of God, and so let us acclaim Christ our Savior.

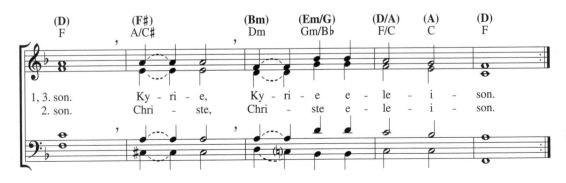

Ideally chanted with minimal or no accompaniment.
Assembly may begin their response on the cantor's last note ("-son.").

GLORY TO GOD

The Glory to God is said or sung on Sundays outside Advent and Lent, on solemnities and feasts, and in solemn local celebrations.

Glory to God in the highest,
   and peace to his people on earth.
Lord God, heavenly King,
almighty God and Father,
   we worship you, we give you thanks,
   we praise you for your glory.
Lord Jesus Christ, only Son of the Father,
Lord God, Lamb of God,
you take away the sin of the world:
   have mercy on us;
you are seated at the right hand of the Father:
   receive our prayer.
For you alone are the Holy One,
you alone are the Lord,
you alone are the Most High,
   Jesus Christ,
   with the Holy Spirit,
   in the glory of God the Father.
Amen.

Glory to God

4

Mass of Glory
Ken Canedo and Bob Hurd

OPENING PRAYER

Let us pray.
After a period of silence, the priest says the opening prayer.
Amen.

LITURGY OF THE WORD

FIRST READING

After the reading the lector says,

The word of the Lord.
Thanks be to God.

RESPONSORIAL PSALM

Choose a psalm response from Psalms & Canticles (#53–96). Select one of the common texts for the liturgical season, or a psalm appropriate to the feast or occasion.

SECOND READING

After the reading the lector says,

The word of the Lord.
Thanks be to God.

The assembly welcomes the proclamation of the gospel by singing (omit if not sung):

A
5

Alleluia! Give the Glory
Gathering or Gospel Acclamation

Text adapted by Ken Canedo and Bob Hurd

Mass of Glory
Ken Canedo

GATHERING VERSES Vs. 1: Mt 18:20; Vs. 2: Jn 15:5

(C) Eb — Cantor or All
(Cm) Ebm

1. Where __ two or three _____ are __ gath - ered _____ in my
2. I __ am the vine _____ and __ you _____ are the

(G) Bb (C/G) Eb/Bb (G) Bb (G7) Bb7 (C) Eb

1. name, _____ there I am _____ in the
2. branch - es. _____ A - bide _____ in __

(A7) C7 (D) F (A7) C7 (D) F (D7) F7
D.S.

1. midst of them; _____ there I'll be.
2. me _____ and __ bear much fruit. _____

GOSPEL VERSES 3-6 Vs. 3: Jn 8:12; Vs. 4: 1 Sm 9:3, Jn 6:69; Vs. 5: Lk 3:4, 6; Vs. 6: Jn 10:14

(C) Eb — Cantor
(Cm) Ebm
(G) Bb
(C/G) Eb/Bb

(Ord. Time) 3. I __ am __ the __ Light _____ of the World; _____
(Ord. Time) 4. Speak, O Lord, __ your __ ser - vant _____ is __ lis - t'ning; _____
(Advent) 5. Pre - pare __ the __ way _____ of the Lord; _____
(Easter) 6. I __ am __ the good shep - herd, _____ says the Lord; _____

(G) Bb (G7) Bb7 (C) Eb (A7) C7

3. _____ ev - 'ry - one _____ who __ fol - lows me __
4. _____ you __ have _____ the __ words _____
5. _____ ev - 'ry - one _____ shall __ see _____
6. _____ I __ know _____ my __ sheep _____

(D) F (A7) C7 (D) F (D7) F7
D.S. al fine

3. __ will __ have the light _____ of life. _____
4. __ of __ ev - er - last - ing life. _____
5. __ the __ sav - ing pow'r _____ of God. _____
6. __ and __ mine _____ know _____ me. _____

GOSPEL VERSES 7, 8   Vs. 7: Lk 24:32; Vs. 8: *Veni Sancte Spiritus*

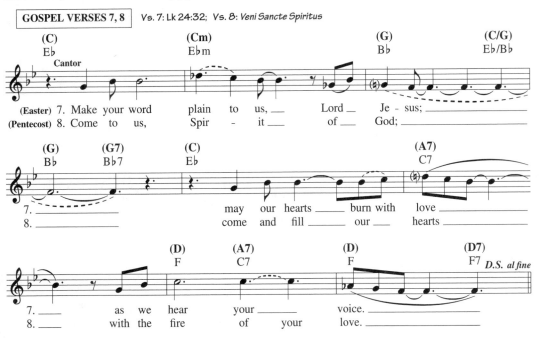

(Easter) 7. Make your word plain to us, Lord __ Je - sus;__
(Pentecost) 8. Come to us, Spir - it __ of __ God;__

7. __ may our hearts __ burn with love __
8. __ come and fill __ our __ hearts __

7. __ as we hear your __ voice.__
8. __ with the fire of your love.__

D.S. al fine

B *(During Lent)*

6

Praise and Honor
Lenten Gospel Acclamation

Mass of Glory
Ken Canedo and Bob Hurd

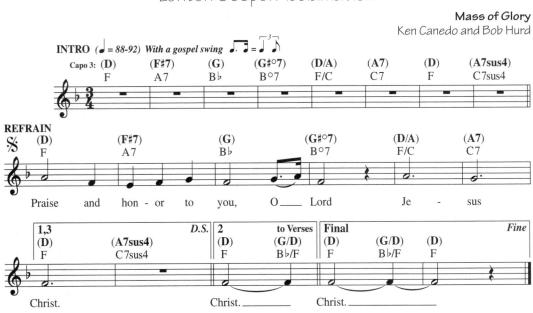

Praise and hon - or to you, O __ Lord Je - sus

Christ.   Christ. __   Christ. __

* Verse numbering indicates the Sunday and cycle of Lent; e.g., "5th C" is the appointed verse for the fifth Sunday of Lent, cycle C.
** Cue notes are an alternative lower melody.

The Order of Mass

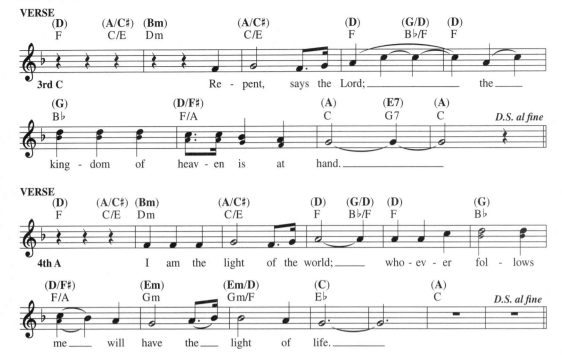

GOSPEL

The Lord be with you.
And also with you.
A reading from the holy gospel according to N.
Glory to you, Lord.
After the reading the priest or deacon says,
The gospel of the Lord.
Praise to you, Lord Jesus Christ.

HOMILY

PROFESSION OF FAITH

On Sundays, solemnities and solemn local celebrations, we recite or sing a creed handed down from the early Church.

A   NICENE CREED

We believe in one God,
   the Father, the Almighty,
   maker of heaven and earth,
   of all that is seen and unseen.
We believe in one Lord, Jesus Christ,
   the only Son of God,
   eternally begotten of the Father,

God from God, Light from Light,
true God from true God,
begotten, not made, one in Being with the Father.
Through him all things were made.
For us men and for our salvation
he came down from heaven:
by the power of the Holy Spirit
he was born of the Virgin Mary, and became man.
For our sake he was crucified under Pontius Pilate;
he suffered, died, and was buried.
On the third day he rose again
in fulfillment of the Scriptures;
he ascended into heaven
and is seated at the right hand of the Father.
He will come again in glory to judge the living and the dead,
and his kingdom will have no end.
We believe in the Holy Spirit, the Lord, the giver of life,
who proceeds from the Father and the Son.
With the Father and the Son he is worshiped and glorified.
He has spoken through the Prophets.
We believe in one holy catholic and apostolic Church.
We acknowledge one baptism for the forgiveness of sins.
We look for the resurrection of the dead,
and the life of the world to come. Amen.

B   APOSTLES' CREED

This creed may be used at Masses with children and youth where only a few adults are present.

I [We] believe in God, the Father almighty,
creator of heaven and earth.
I [We] believe in Jesus Christ, his only Son, our Lord.
He was conceived by the power of the Holy Spirit
and born of the Virgin Mary.
He suffered under Pontius Pilate,
was crucified, died, and was buried.
He descended to the dead.
On the third day he rose again.
He ascended into heaven,
and is seated at the right hand of the Father.
He will come again to judge the living and the dead.
I [We] believe in the Holy Spirit,
the holy catholic Church,
the communion of saints,
the forgiveness of sins,
the resurrection of the body,
and the life everlasting. Amen.

GENERAL INTERCESSIONS

To each petition all respond in these or similar words:

Lord, hear our prayer.

7 (Setting 1 – Hear Our Prayer)

Mass of Glory
Ken Canedo and Bob Hurd

Play Response as an Intro.

8 (Setting 2 – God of Mercy)

Mass of Glory
Bob Hurd

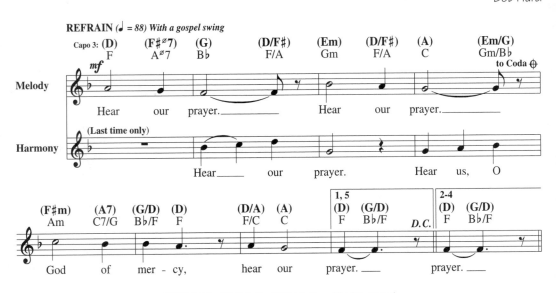

Play Refrain as an Intro.

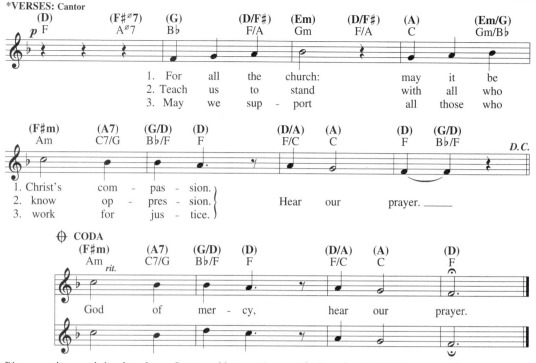

*Verses may be expanded or altered according to need. Intercessions may also be spoken, with quiet instrumental accompaniment.

After the petitions, the priest says the concluding prayer:

Amen.

LITURGY OF THE EUCHARIST

PREPARATION OF THE ALTAR AND THE GIFTS

If there is no music or song, the following prayers may be said aloud:

Blessed are you, Lord…
Blessed be God for ever.

PRAYER OVER THE GIFTS

Pray, brethren, that our sacrifice may be acceptable to God,
the almighty Father.
May the Lord accept the sacrifice at your hands
for the praise and glory of his name,
for our good, and the good of all his Church.
The priest says the prayer over the gifts, and all respond:
Amen.

INTRODUCTORY DIALOGUE

9

Mass of Glory
Ken Canedo and Bob Hurd

PREFACE

The priest recites or sings an introductory prayer for this feast or occasion.

HOLY

Mass of Glory
Ken Canedo and Bob Hurd

The Order of Mass

MEMORIAL ACCLAMATION

Mass of Glory
Ken Canedo and Bob Hurd

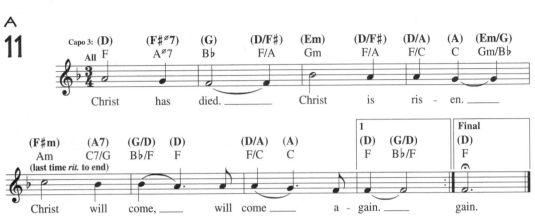

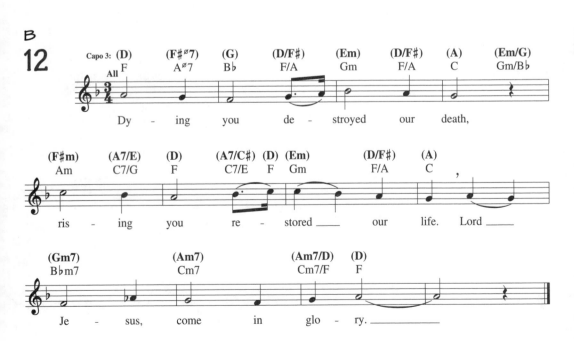

When invitation is spoken, Intro may begin here.

C

When we eat this bread ___ and ___ drink ___ this cup, we pro-claim your death, Lord Je-sus, ___ un-til you come in glo-ry, un-til you come in glo-ry. ___

D

Lord, by your cross and res-ur-rec-tion ___ you have set us free. ___ You are the Sav-ior, ___ the Sav-ior of the world. ___

(Setting 1)

Mass of Glory
Ken Canedo and Bob Hurd

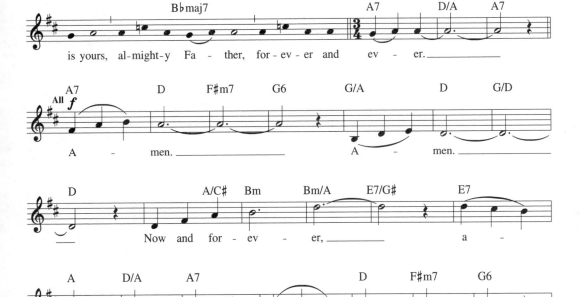

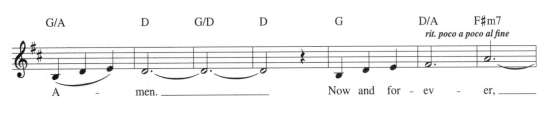

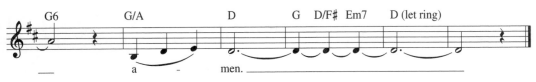

COMMUNION RITE

LORD'S PRAYER

17

Mass of Glory
Ken Canedo and Bob Hurd

Priest

Let us pray for the coming of the king-dom as Je - sus taught us:

Capo 3: **(D)**
F

(A)
C

All: Our Father, who art in heaven,
All: Give us this day our daily bread; and forgive us our trespasses
Priest: Deliver us, Lord, from every evil, and grant us peace in our day.
*All: For the kingdom, the power, and the glo - ry are yours,

(Em)
Gm

(D/F♯) **(A7)** **(D)**
F/A C7 F

hallow - éd be thy name;
as we forgive those who tres - pass a - gainst us;
In your mercy keep us free from sin and protect us from all an - xiety
the kingdom, the power, and the glo - ry are yours,

(F♯)
A/C♯

(Bm) **(Em/G)**
Dm Gm/B♭

1-3
(D/A)
F/C

(A)
C

(D)
F

thy kingdom come; thy will be done on earth as it is in heaven.
and lead us not in - to temp-tation, but de - liver us from evil.
as we wait in joyful hope for the coming of our Savior, Jesus Christ.
the kingdom, the power, and the glory are yours,

Final
(D/A)
F/C

(F♯7)
A7/C♯

(Bm)
Dm

(Em/G)
Gm/B♭

(D/A)
F/C

(A7)
C7

(D)
F

now and for - ev - er, _____ now and for - ev - er.

Ideally, the chanted portion of this setting is done with minimal or no accompaniment.
* "For the kingdom..." may be sung in chant style, or in $\frac{12}{8}$ meter (next page).

SIGN OF PEACE

Lord Jesus Christ . . . where you live for ever and ever.

Amen.

The peace of the Lord be with you always.

And also with you.

Let us offer each other the sign of peace.

BREAKING OF THE BREAD

The eucharistic bread is broken and the consecrated wine poured in preparation for communion. The following is sung throughout this action:

18

Lamb of God
(Setting 1)

Mass of Glory
Bob Hurd

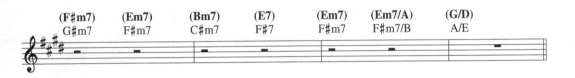

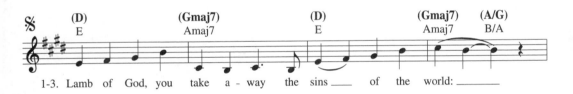

1-3. Lamb of God, you take a - way the sins ___ of the world:

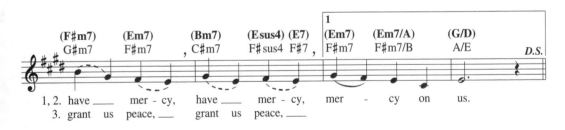

1, 2. have ___ mer - cy, have ___ mer - cy, mer - cy on us.
3. grant us peace, ___ grant us peace, ___

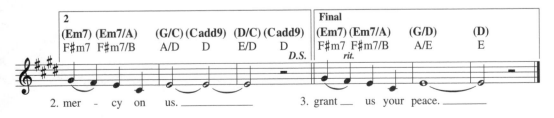

2. mer - cy on us. ___   3. grant ___ us your peace. ___

Lamb of God

(Setting 2)

Mass of Glory
Bob Hurd

More invocations may be added as needed: Son of God, Promise of Life, etc.

COMMUNION

This is the Lamb of God who takes away the sins of the world.
Happy are those who are called to his supper.
Lord, I am not worthy to receive you,
but only say the word and I shall be healed.

The minister of communion says, "The body of Christ" or "The blood of Christ," and the communicant answers:

Amen.

COMMUNION SONG

Choose a song from Communion Songs (#149–167) or Psalms & Canticles (#53–96).

PERIOD OF SILENCE OR SONG OF PRAISE

A period of silence may now be observed, or a psalm or song of praise may be sung.

PRAYER AFTER COMMUNION

Let us pray…
Amen.

CONCLUDING RITE

GREETING AND BLESSING

The Lord be with you.
And also with you.
May almighty God bless you, the Father, and the Son, and the Holy Spirit.
Amen.

(The priest may choose another solemn blessing or prayer over the people).

DISMISSAL

A   Go in the peace of Christ.
B   The Mass is ended, go in peace.
C   Go in peace to love and serve the Lord.
     Thanks be to God.

CLOSING SONG (SENDING FORTH OR RECESSIONAL)

Choose a final psalm (#53–96), hymn (#97–148), or song of praise (#168–213).

GUIDELINES FOR THE RECEPTION OF COMMUNION

For Catholics: As Catholics, we fully participate in the celebration of the Eucharist when we receive Holy Communion. We are encouraged to receive Communion devoutly and frequently. In order to be properly disposed to receive Communion, participants should not be conscious of grave sin and normally should have fasted for one hour. A person who is conscious of grave sin is not to receive the Body and Blood of the Lord without prior sacramental confession except for a grave reason where there is no opportunity for confession. In this case, the person is to be mindful of the obligation to make an act of perfect contrition, including the intention of confessing as soon as possible (Code of Canon Law, canon 916). A frequent reception of the Sacrament of Penance is encouraged for all.

For our fellow Christians: We welcome our fellow Christians to this celebration of the Eucharist as our brothers and sisters. We pray that our common baptism and the action of the Holy Spirit in this Eucharist will draw us closer to one another and begin to dispel the sad divisions which separate us. We pray that these will lessen and finally disappear, in keeping with Christ's prayer for us "that they may all be one" (Jn 17:21).

Because Catholics believe that the celebration of the Eucharist is a sign of the reality of the oneness of faith, life, and worship, members of those churches with whom we are not yet fully united are ordinarily not admitted to Holy Communion. Eucharistic sharing in exceptional circumstances by other Christians requires permission according to the directives of the diocesan bishop and the provisions of canon law (canon 844 ¶ 4). Members of the Orthodox Churches, the Assyrian Church of the East, and the Polish National Catholic Church are urged to respect the discipline of their own Churches. According to Roman Catholic discipline, the Code of Canon Law does not object to the reception of communion by Christians of these Churches (canon 844 ¶ 3).

For those not receiving Holy Communion: All who are not receiving Holy Communion are encouraged to express in their hearts a prayerful desire for unity with the Lord Jesus and with one another.

For non-Christians: We also welcome to this celebration those who do not share our faith in Jesus Christ. While we cannot admit them to Holy Communion, we ask them to offer their prayers for the peace and the unity of the human family.

GUIDE TO PREPARING MASS

Here is a guide to prepare Mass especially on occasions when many youth and young adults will be present. Remember, the Mass as a whole never changes, so there is no need to plan it. Our job is to prepare the Word, the rituals, the environment, the music, and ourselves, so that all people gathered on this occasion will be able to participate fully, consciously, and actively. Be sure to leave plenty of room for the Holy Spirit to guide our prayer and participation!

FORM A PREPARATION TEAM AND CHOOSE A LEADER

The Mass is Christ's work in which we, the members of the Body of Christ, join in celebrating. By its nature, the Mass is a communal prayer. It is therefore always best whenever possible to involve several persons in the preparation, especially the priest who will preside. A Liturgy Preparation Team that works together regularly is able to learn from its past efforts to help the community pray more fully. The team leader is responsible for leading the session, keeping everyone on task and involved, and communicating with the priest if he is not present.

GATHER PREPARATION RESOURCES

Gather all the necessary resources. You will need:

- the *Lectionary* (book of readings) or copies of the readings for team members
- the *Sacramentary* (book of prayers and rituals)
- *Spirit & Song* and other music resources
- Mass preparation forms, pens, etc.
- Check other sacristy necessities such as chalice, communion vessels, hosts and wine, candles, altar cloth, etc.
- Check availability of microphones, music stands, etc.

DISCUSS THE CONTEXT FOR THIS MASS

The people present, the time, the place and the surrounding events make every Mass unique. It is important that the team discuss the context of each liturgy so that it can prepare the Word, the music, and the rituals for full participation. Here are several simple questions to think about and discuss:

WHO is likely to be present at this Mass? How diverse in age and culture will the group be? How well do they know each other? Are there any other special circumstances that will affect their attention and participation? (Example: a retreat group, certain visitors, etc.)

WHAT local or world events will influence or shape the prayer and participation of those gathered for this Mass? Are there any particular needs for prayer? (Example: a local tragedy, an anniversary, a feast or special occasion.)

WHERE will the Mass take place? Are there particular advantages or limitations to keep in mind? (Example: a large church for a small group, no official chapel at the retreat site.)

WHEN will the Mass take place? What time of day? Is this a regularly scheduled liturgy or a special occasion? What is the liturgical feast or season? Is this a special season or calendar holiday? (Example: World Youth Day, Fourth of July, local graduations, at a conference, late evening versus an early morning Mass, etc.)

REFLECT ON THE SCRIPTURES

Read and reflect on the scriptures assigned for this day, keeping in mind the contexts the team has just identified. Read the gospel first. It will set the stage to hear the first and second readings. As necessary, review other sources for additional background information on the passages. Discuss how these readings apply to the group who will gather for this Mass.

Special Note: *Always use the assigned readings of the day. If you need to choose other readings because of the nature of the group or event, first check the votive and ritual Masses in the back of the Lectionary for suggestions rather than selecting passages directly from scripture. The priest who will preside should be involved in selecting these readings.*

IDENTIFY A FOCUS FOR PREPARATION

Several key ideas will emerge as you discuss the scriptures in the context of this Mass. Summarize those ideas into several words or a short phrase that can be used to focus the rest of your planning and preparation. Remember, every Mass has the same theme—the Paschal Mystery that Christ has died, Christ is risen, Christ will come again. Focus your preparation toward helping the assembly pray and participate more fully.

PREPARE THE ELEMENTS OF MASS

Three sets of tasks need to be accomplished. Work together or in teams.

Readings and Prayer Tasks

• Determine who will be lectors and how the scriptures will be proclaimed.

• Review the Sacramentary prayers. Make any necessary suggestions to the presider.

• Compose or prepare the prayer of the faithful. Determine who will present it. (Check with the music group if the response will be sung.)

• Prepare texts or prayers for any special blessings or rituals. (Example: commissioning a team leaving on a service event, a blessing prayer on World Youth Day, etc.)

• (Optional) Share the notes from your preparation with the priest/presider, homilist and musicians. This may be particularly helpful to someone who is unfamiliar with the group or occasion.

Music and Song Tasks

• Choose a Mass setting from #20–40, or the *Mass of Glory* included in the Order of Mass.

• Choose a Responsorial Psalm from #53–92. See the psalm tables on p.100 and p.188 for suggestions.

• Choose songs for gathering and sending forth from #97–148.

• Choose a song for the Communion procession from #149–167, or a psalm from #53–92.

• Select other ritual music or songs for the penitential rite or sprinkling rite, preparation of the altar and the gifts, or blessings from #20–52.

• Consider choosing music or songs to play prior to the start of Mass, for praise or to practice with the assembly.

• Prepare hymnals or additional song sheets for the assembly. Secure necessary copyrights.

• Set up the sound equipment, music stands, and other related tasks.

Rituals and Environment Tasks

- Prepare the church or arrange the place where Mass will be celebrated.

- Prepare the altar and ambo with appropriate cloths, candles, Lectionary, and Sacramentary.

- Prepare the hosts, water and wine, communion vessels, purificators, and vestments.

- Decorate with appropriate and seasonal art, flowers, plants, cloths or cultural artifacts.

- Prepare any processions, liturgical movement, or ritual gestures.

- Plan for how the gifts will be presented.

- Assign Eucharistic ministers and plan how the Holy Communion will be distributed.

- Make a plan for greeting the assembly before and after Mass, for distributing songbooks or the order of worship, and for arranging the chairs (if necessary).

REVIEW THE OVERALL PLAN

The Mass is the responsibility of everyone gathered. Make sure your preparations allow for people to pray together, not to be prayed at! Most importantly, leave room for God to speak to your team, so that Mass can be your prayer as well. Some final tasks to keep in mind:

- Review the work of each task group

- Meet with the priest/presider and review the order of worship

- Rehearse readings, music cues, processions, etc.

- Pray as a team

EVALUATE THE MASS

Evaluation is the last step of preparing Mass. Take time at the beginning of your next meeting to ask, did our preparations help the people to pray? Evaluation is not a time to list the ways things went wrong but to review if your preparations were successful in helping the assembly to pray more fully. Celebrate the successes and learn from the mistakes.

MASS OF A JOYFUL HEART

20 Glory to God

Mass of a Joyful Heart
Steve Angrisano and Tom Tomaszek

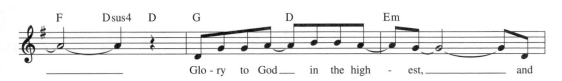

Glo - ry to God __ in the high - est, _____ and peace to his peo - ple on earth. __

_____ Glo - ry to God __ in the high - est, _____ and

peace to his peo - ple on earth. __

1. Lord God, heav - en - ly King, al -

1. might - y God __ and Fa - ther, _____ we wor - ship you, we give you

1. thanks, we praise you for __ your glo - ry. _____

21

Alleluia
Gospel Acclamation

Mass of a Joyful Heart
Steve Angrisano

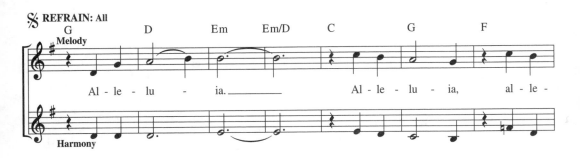

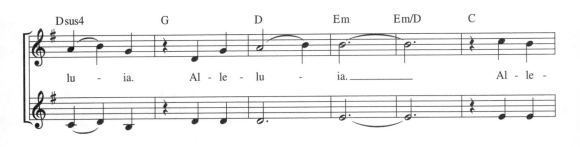

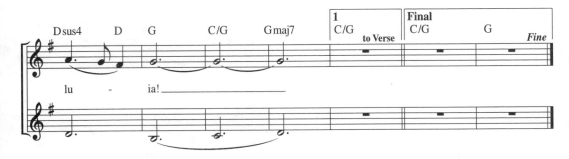

VERSES: Cantor

(Ordinary Time) 1. Let your heart re - joice in the Lord.
(Pentecost) 2. God will send his Spir - it to you.

1. Let your word pro - claim his deeds._____ Let your
2. He will teach you all his truths._____ Ho - ly

1. voice sing out to the world that our God has
2. Spir - it, shine_____ on us the_____ ra - diance

1. come to save._____
2. of your light._____

D.S. al fine

22

Holy

Mass of a Joyful Heart

Steve Angrisano and Tom Tomaszek

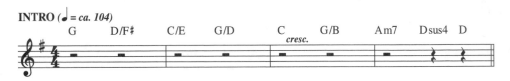

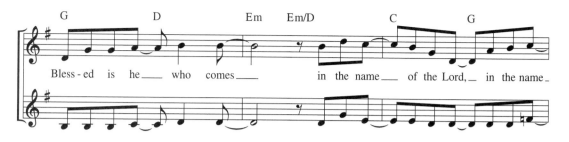

Bless - ed is he ___ who comes ___ in the name ___ of the Lord, ___ in the name ___

___ of the Lord. ___ Ho - san - na in ___ the high - est, ___

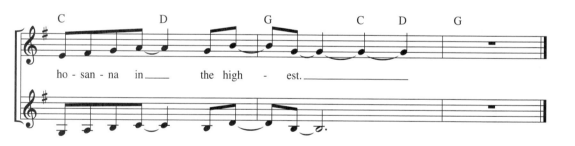

ho - san - na in ___ the high - est. ___

23

Christ Has Died
Memorial Acclamation A

Mass of a Joyful Heart
Steve Angrisano and Tom Tomaszek

Dying You Destroyed Our Death 24
Memorial Acclamation B

Mass of a Joyful Heart
Steve Angrisano

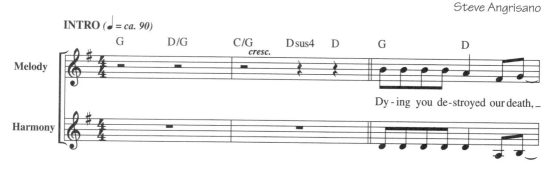

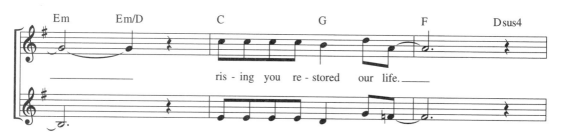

25

Amen

Mass of a Joyful Heart
Steve Angrisano

Lamb of God

Mass of a Joyful Heart
Steve Angrisano

MASS OF LIFE

27

Glory to God

Mass of Life
Tom Booth

*Capo 1 begins at final refrain.

FINAL REFRAIN

Alleluia

29 Profession of Faith

Mass of Life
Tom Booth

Refrain text by Terry Bolduc

INTRO (♩ = ca. 78)

VERSE 1

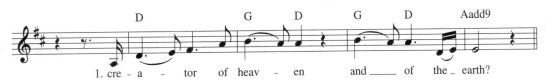

1. Do you be-lieve in God, the Fa - ther Al - might - y,

1. cre - a - tor of heav - en and _____ of the earth?

℞ REFRAIN

A - men, a - men! A - men, a - men!

A - men— we do be - lieve! _____

VERSE 2

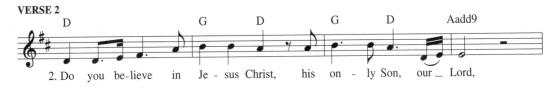

2. Do you be-lieve in Je - sus Christ, his on - ly Son, our Lord,

2. who was born of the Vir-gin Ma - ry, was cru - ci-fied and died, and was

*Capo 1 begins at Verse 3.

Holy

Mass of Life
Tom Booth
Arranged by Tom Booth and Trevor Thomson

Ho - ly, ho - ly, ho - ly Lord, God of pow'r and might,_____

heav'n and earth are full of your glo - ry. Ho - san - na in the

high - est.____ Ho - san - na on high. Ho - san - na on

high. Blessed is he who comes in the name, in the name of the

Lord. Ho - san - na in the high - est. Ho - san - na on

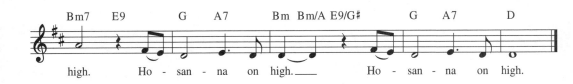

high. Ho - san - na on high.____ Ho - san - na on high.

Memorial Acclamation A

Mass of Life
Tom Booth

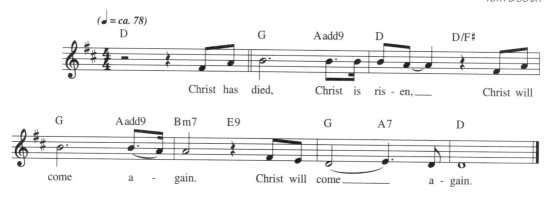

Christ has died, Christ is ris-en, ___ Christ will
come a - gain. Christ will come ___ a - gain.

Amen

Mass of Life
Tom Booth

A - men, a - men, a -
men, a - men. A - men, we do be - lieve.
A - men, ___ a - men.

MISA DEL MUNDO

Pronunciation Guide

KYRIE

Greek Kyrie eleison
kee-ree-eh eh-leh-ee-sohn

Greek Christe eleison
kree-steh eh-leh-ee-sohn

ALLELUIA

Chamoru Jesus hagu ham muna fan lala'la'
hay-soos hah-goo hahm moo-nah fahn lah-lah-lah

Chamoru I haga'-mu muna fan libre ham
ee hah-gah-moo moo-nah fahn lee-bree hahm

TUHAN DENGAR DOA KAMI (O GOD, HEAR OUR PRAYER)

Indonesian Tuhan dengar doa kami
Too-hahn dehng-ar doh-ah kah-mee

'OKU, 'OKU, MA'ONI'ONI (HOLY, HOLY GOD)

Tongan 'Oku, 'oku, ma'oni'oni
oh-koo oh-koo mah-oh-nee-oh-nee

Spanish Santo, santo es El Señor
sahn-toh sahn-toh ehs el Seh-nyor

Tagalog Santo, santong panginoong Diyos
sahn-toh sahn-tonng pahng-ee-noo-ohng dee-yos

Polish Swiety! Swiety Boze
*shvee-ehn-tih shvee-ehn-tih boh-'j'uh

* 'j' is pronounced like the 's' in measure, but softer

(continued on p. 68)

Kyrie

Misa del Mundo
Jesse Manibusan

34 Glory to God Most High

Misa del Mundo
Jesse Manibusan

Play Refrain as an Intro.

35

Alleluia

Misa del Mundo

Jesse Manibusan

Jesse Manibusan and Tony Gómez

VERSE 1

VERSE 2

FINAL REFRAIN: All

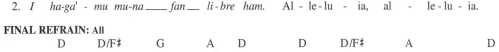

Tuhan Dengar Doa Kami

(O God, Hear Our Prayer)

Misa del Mundo
Jesse Manibusan

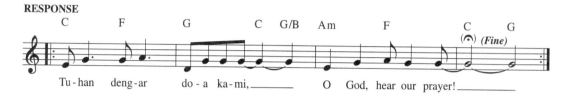

Tu - han deng - ar do - a ka - mi,_____ O God, hear our prayer!_____

(Deacon, Cantor, or other person)

That we might be a Church of prayer and action,
to dismantle the violence and break down the barriers of prejudice and racism.
We pray to the Lord. (Response)

Rogamos por nosotros para que seamos una iglesia de oración y acción,
que desarma la violencia y quiebra las barreras del prejuicio y el racismo.
Oramos al Señor. (Response)

For our leaders, that they may be committed to truth and integrity
as they lead us into the future and speak for those whose lives are voiceless
due to racism, sexism and discrimination.
We pray to the Lord. (Response)

Rogamos por nuestros líderes, que se entreguen a la verdad y a la integridad
mientras nos guían al futuro y hablan por aquellos cuyas vidas no tiene voz,
por motivo del racismo, el sexismo y la discriminación.
Oramos al Señor. (Response)

37 'Oku, 'Oku Ma'oni'oni

(Holy, Holy God)

Misa del Mundo
Jesse Manibusan

'O - ku, 'o - ku ma - 'o - ni - 'o - ni! ___ 'O - ku, 'o - ku ma -

'o - ni - 'o - ni! ___ ¡San - to, san - to es El Se - ñor! _____

___ ¡San - to, san - to es El Se - ñor! _____ *Heav-en and earth ___ are full ___*

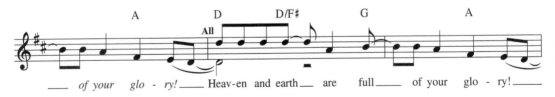

___ *of your glo - ry! ___ Heav-en and earth ___ are full ___ of your glo - ry! ___*

___ *San - to, san - tong pang - i - noo - ng Diyos! _____ San - to, san - tong pang - i -*

noo - ng Diyos! _ Św - ie - ty! ___ Św - ie - ty Bo - że! _ Św - ie -

CRISTO HA MUERTO (CHRIST HAS DIED)

Spanish Cristo ha muerto **kree-stoh ah mwehr-toh**
Tagalog si Kristo'y nabuhay **see kree-sto-ee nah-boo-high**

CANTAMOS AMEN (WE SING AMEN)

Spanish Cantamos amén **kahn-tah-mohs ah-meyhn**
Tagalog Sumasampalataya **soo-mah-sahm-pah-lah-tah-ee-yah**

LẠY CHIÊN THIÊN CHÚA (LAMB OF GOD)

Vietnamese Lạy chiên Thiên Chúa **lie chee-én tee-én joowah**
(Alternative Tagalog Lyric: Kordero ng Diyos **kor-deh-roh nahng deeyohs**)

MALO! MALO! THANKS BE TO GOD (song #129)

Refrain
Tongan Malo Malo **mah-loh mah-loh**
Portuguese Obrigado **o-bree-ga-doh**
Spanish Gracias **grah-seeahs**
Korean Kam sa ham ni da **kahm sah hahm nee dah**

Verse 1
Chamoru Si Yu'us maa'se **see joos mah-ah-sih**
Indonesian Terima kasih **three-mah kah-seeh**
Tagalog Maraming salamat **mah-rah-meeng sah-lah-maht**
German Danke schön **dahn-kuh shuh(r)n**
Polish Dziękuję **jehn-koo-yeh**

Verse 2
Creole Mèsi bokou **meh-see boh-koo**
Mandarin Xie xie **shee-eh shee-eh**
Japanese Arigatō **ah-ree-gah-toh**
Italian Grazie **grah-tsee-eh**
Vietnamese Cám ờn **gahm urn**

Cristo Ha Muerto

(Christ Has Died — Memorial Acclamation A)

Misa del Mundo
Jesse Manibusan

Mass Settings & Ritual Music

39

Cantamos Amen

(We Sing Amen)

Misa del Mundo
Jesse Manibusan

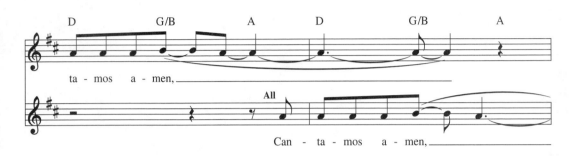

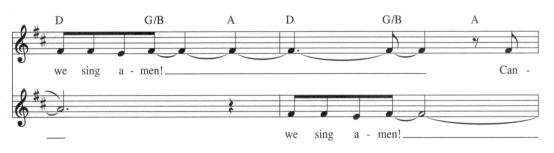

40 Lạy Chiên Thiên Chúa
(Lamb of God)

Misa del Mundo
Jesse Manibusan

Streams of Living Water
(Sprinkling Rite)

41

Based on Ezekiel 47:1; John 7:38; Revelation 7:17

Cyprian Consiglio

42

Kyrie

Jeffrey Roscoe

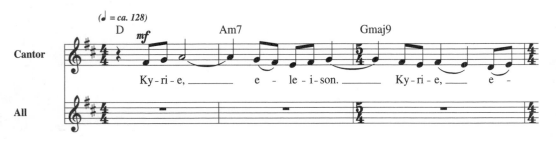

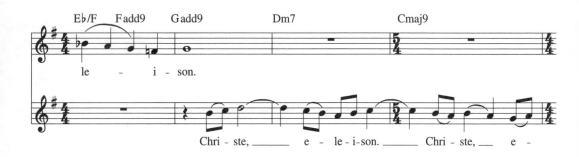

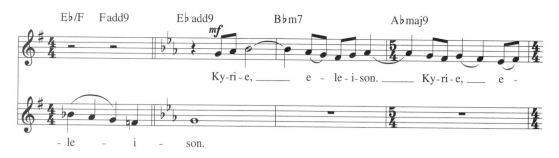

43 Glory to God

Fr. Richard Ho Lung, M.O.P.
Caribbean Mass
Arranged by Jon and Wynton Williams

*Capo 1 begins at key change.

Advent/Christmas Gospel Acclamation

44

David Haas

Play Refrain as an Intro.

45 Celtic Alleluia

Fintan O'Carroll / Christopher Walker

ALTERNATIVE VERSES
Te Deum

VERSES

1. ᵞ Fa - ther, we praise you as Lord, _____ all of the earth gives you wor-ship,
2. ᵞ Bless - ed a - pos - tles sing praise; _____ proph - ets and mar - tyrs give glo - ry:
3. ᵞ You are the Christ ev - er - last-ing, _____ born for us all of a Vir - gin,
4. ᵞ Help those you saved by your blood, _____ raise them to life with your mar-tyrs.

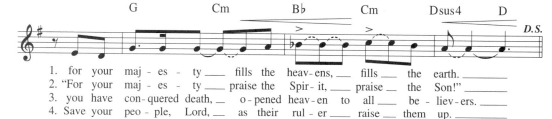

1. for your maj - es - ty ___ fills the heav-ens, ___ fills ___ the earth. _____
2. "For your maj - es - ty ___ praise the Spir - it, ___ praise ___ the Son!" _____
3. you have con-quered death, _ o - pened heav-en to all ___ be - liev-ers. _____
4. Save your peo - ple, Lord, _ as their rul - er ____ raise ___ them up. _____

Advent
> Stay awake, pray at all times,
> praying that you may be strengthened,
> that with confidence
> you can meet the Son of Man.

Christmas Day
> "I bring you news of great joy,
> joy for all nations,
> for today is born
> our savior, Christ the Lord."

Holy Family
> The Word of God became flesh
> and came to dwell among us.
> All accepting him
> will become children of God.

Epiphany
> A holy day has dawned.
> Adore the Lord, you nations,
> for today a light
> has come on the earth.

Easter
1. Give thanks to the Lord, who is good.
   The love of the Lord knows no ending.
   All in Israel say,
   "God's love has no end."

2. The Right Hand of God raised me up.
   The hand of the Lord has triumphed.
   I shall never die,
   I shall live, telling God's deeds.

3. The stone which the builders rejected,
   becomes the cornerstone chosen.
   Praise the work of God
   for this marvel in our eyes.

Pentecost
> Come, Holy Spirit.
> Fill the hearts of your faithful
> and enlighten them
> with the fire of your love.

Wedding
1. If we love one another,
   if we love one another,
   God will live in us,
   and that love will be strong.

2. All those who live in love
   with God are united,
   for they live with God
   and God lives in them.

3. Dear friends, God is love.
   So let us love one another.
   Being one with God,
   as God loves us, let us love.

Feasts of Mary
> Hail: full of grace,
> Mary, most blessed among women;
> who believed that it
> would be as God promised.

46 Glory and Praise
(Lenten Gospel Acclamation)

Jesse Manibusan

Litany of Saints

Grayson Warren Brown
Arranged by Larry Adams

*   Accompaniment is optional. If used, chords in brackets may be omitted.
** Continue with other names, such as: Saint Joseph, Saint Peter, Saint John, Saint Augustine, Saint Cecilia, Holy Martyrs, Ugandan saints, Brother Martin King, Saint de Porres.
*** Continue with other phrases such as: "That we might be more loving," "That we might build your kingdom," "That we might end all hatred," "That we might preach the Good News," "That we might feel the Holy Ghost."

Mass Settings & Ritual Music

48

Hear Our Prayer

(General Intercessions)

Tom Tomaszek

INTRO (♩ = ca. 100)

*Am   Em7   Fmaj7   G

(Keybd)

VERSES 1-4

Am   Em7   F   C   G

1. God of___ the ag - es, ___ we look___ to you ___
2. God of___ the suf - f'ring, ___ hear us, ___ we pray. ___
3. God of___ the search - ing, ___ hear us, ___ we pray. ___
4. God of___ the bro - ken, ___ hear us, ___ we pray. ___

Am   Em7   F   Esus4   E

1. to guide___ all lead - ers ___ to seek___ your truth. ___
2. Com-fort___ your peo - ple, ___ hold us___ to you. ___
3. Guide us___ in safe - ty ___ and lead___ us home. ___
4. Nour-ish___ our hun - gers ___ and heal___ our hearts. ___

REFRAIN

Am Melody   Em7   Am

Hear our prayer, ___ hear our prayer. ___

Harmony

Lord, hear our prayer. ___

Em7   Am   Em7

Hear our prayer, ___ Lord, hear our prayer. ___

___ Lord, hear our prayer. ___

F   E   Am

Hear our prayer. ___

*Capo 1 begins at verse 5.

49

Our Father

Steve Croskey
Arranged by Tim Smith

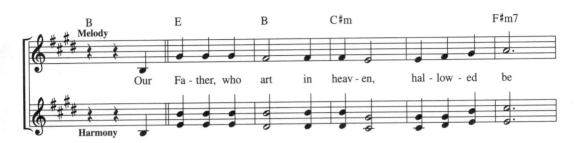

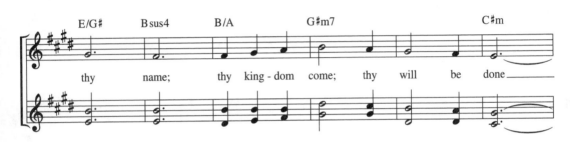

Priest: Deliver us, Lord, from every evil, and grant us peace in our day.
In your mercy keep us free from sin and protect us from all anxiety
as we wait in joyful hope for the coming of our Savior, Jesus Christ.

87

50

Lamb of God

Bobby Fisher

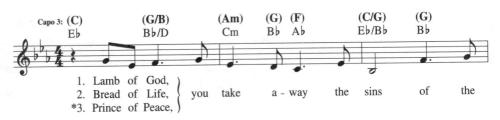

1. Lamb of God,
2. Bread of Life,   you take a - way the sins of the
*3. Prince of Peace,

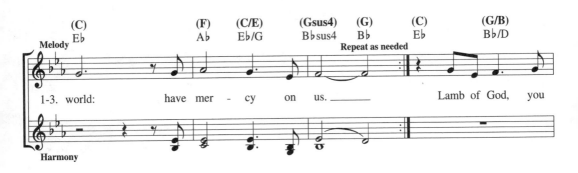

1-3. world: have mer - cy on us. _____   Lamb of God, you

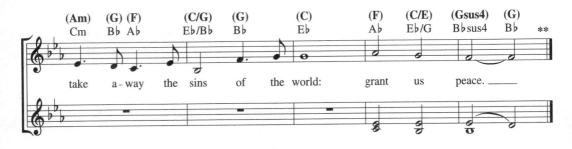

take a - way the sins of the world: grant us peace. _____

Play first six measures as an Intro.

*Additional invocations: Cup of Hope, Word of God, etc.
**This song may lead directly into the Communion song, "Bread of Life," song number 150.

Radiant Light Divine

(Phos Hilaron)

51

Based on *Phos Hilaron*, Greek ca. 200

Rufino Zaragoza, OFM

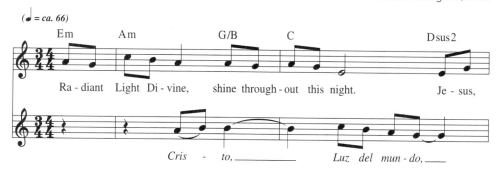

*omit F♯

52

There Is a Light
(Lucernarium)

Cyprian Consiglio

There is a light that can o-ver-come the dark-ness. There is no dark-ness that can o-ver-come the light. light.

1. Cre - a - tor of un - fail - ing light, __ give that same light to 1. those who call __ you. __ May our lives pro-claim your

*Guitar accompaniment is optional.

1. good-ness, our voic - es sing your praise for - ev - er! _____

VERSE 2

2. Lord Je - sus Christ, ___ you are the true light of the

2. world. _____ Give us cour-age, strength and grace to

2. build a world of jus - tice and _____ peace. _____

VERSE 3

3. May the light of the Ho - ly Spir - it dis - pel the

3. dark-ness of our times. _____ Turn our ha - tred in - to

3. love, our wars in - to the peace we so ___ de - sire. _____

MORNING PRAYER

Christians dedicate the day to God by celebrating the Liturgy of the Hours in the Holy Spirit through Christ. Our Morning Prayer is filled with praise to God for life, and for all the blessings of the day, regardless of any difficulties we may face. Before we begin, take a moment of personal prayer to remember the many ways God has blessed us with friends, family, and abilities to "live life to its fullest" (John 10:10).

OPENING DIALOGUE

Trace the Sign of the Cross on your lips as the leader begins the prayer.

> Lord, open my lips.
> **And my mouth will proclaim your praise.**

MORNING HYMN

Choose an appropriate hymn or song from Gathering & Sending Songs (#97–148) or Psalms & Canticles (#53–96). Psalm 95 (#73) is commonly used as a Morning Hymn.

PSALM

Choose from #53–92. Psalm 63 (#68) is commonly used for Morning Prayer. If the psalm is not sung, designate two sides and alternate reciting the verses. Repeat the antiphon at the beginning and end.

PSALM PRAYER

> Let us pray.
> *Pause for silent prayer.*
> As morning breaks, Lord, we look to you for strength, guidance and courage. Make us strong today in our desire to live the Gospel. Guide our decisions and actions as we strive to follow you. Give us the courage today to be witnesses of your incredible mercy and love.
> We ask this through Christ, our Lord.
> **Amen.**

READING

After the reading the lector says,

> The word of the Lord.
> **Thanks be to God.**

REFLECTION ON THE WORD OF GOD / HOMILY

Reflect in silence after the reading. A short homily may also be added.

GOSPEL CANTICLE: BENEDICTUS

The Canticle of Zachary may be sung or recited. Choose from setting #93 or 94.

INTERCESSIONS

Let us offer our prayers to God, who hears the cry of the poor.
To each petition all respond in these or similar words:
Lord, hear our prayer.

LORD'S PRAYER

Let us pray as Jesus taught us:
Our Father…
For the kingdom, the power, and the glory are yours, now and forever.
Amen.

CONCLUDING PRAYER

Gracious God, you are truly awesome. You are the Way we strive to follow,
the Truth we always seek, and the Life we long to share forever.
May our hearts always seek you. May our lives proclaim your justice.
May our voices tell the glory of your most holy name.
We make this prayer through Christ, our Lord, who lives and reigns with you,
One God, the Father, the Son, and the Holy Spirit, now and forever.
Amen.

DISMISSAL

May the Lord bless us, protect us from all evil,
and bring us to everlasting life.
Amen.
Let us share a sign of Christ's peace with one another.

CLOSING SONG (OPTIONAL)

Choose a final song or hymn from #97–148 or sing additional verses of the Morning Hymn,
if appropriate.

EVENING PRAYER

Christians gather in the evening to give thanks to God for the day that is ending. Our Evening Prayer is filled with gratitude for the ways God has carried our burdens and made our path brighter by the light of Jesus Christ. Before we begin, take a moment of personal prayer to give thanks to God for the simple blessings of the day, for the people who have helped us to know the Lord, and for a peaceful night.

OPENING DIALOGUE

Make the Sign of the Cross as the leader begins the prayer.

> God, come to my assistance.
> **O Lord, make haste to help me.**
> Glory be to the Father, and to the Son, and to the Holy Spirit,
> **as it was in the beginning, is now, and will be forever. Amen.**

CANDLE LIGHTING (LUCERNARIUM)

Evening prayer may also begin by lighting a candle and processing with it to welcome the evening. The following (or similar) antiphon is either spoken or sung (consider singing #52).

> Light and peace in our Lord, Jesus Christ.
> **Thanks be to God. (Alleluia.)**

EVENING HYMN (PHOS HILARON)

Choose song #51 or another appropriate hymn or song from Gathering & Sending Songs (#97–148) or Psalms & Canticles (#53–96).

PSALM

Choose from #53–92. Psalm 141 (#90) is commonly used for Evening Prayer. If the psalm is not sung, designate two sides and alternate reciting the verses. Repeat the antiphon at the beginning and end.

PSALM PRAYER

> Let us pray.
> *Pause for silent prayer.*
> From the beginning of the day until its ending, we are grateful for the light of your love. Jesus, the Word made flesh, is a lamp unto our feet and a light for our path. Thank you for watching over us even when we lose our way. Thank you for your constant love. Complete in us the work of your love and bring us to life. We make this prayer through Christ, our Lord.
> **Amen.**

READING

After the reading the lector says,

> The word of the Lord.
> **Thanks be to God.**

REFLECTION ON THE WORD OF GOD / HOMILY

Reflect in silence after the reading. A short homily may also be added.

GOSPEL CANTICLE: MAGNIFICAT

The Canticle of Mary can be sung or recited. Choose from setting #95 or 96.

INTERCESSIONS

> Let us offer our prayers and thanks to God.
> *To each petition all respond in these or similar words:*
> **Lord, hear our prayer.**

LORD'S PRAYER

> Let us pray as Jesus taught us:
> **Our Father…**
> For the kingdom, the power, and the glory are yours, now and forever.
> **Amen.**

CONCLUDING PRAYER

> Loving God, you are light in our darkness, a beacon of hope for all to see.
> The power of your love changes our hearts and illuminates our world.
> **May our eyes always be fixed upon you. May our good works give you glory.**
> **May our hearts be one with you, this night and for all our days.**
> We make this prayer through Christ, our Lord, who lives and reigns with you,
> One God, the Father, the Son, and the Holy Spirit, now and forever.
> **Amen.**

DISMISSAL

> May the Lord bless us, protect us from all evil, and bring us to everlasting life.
> **Amen.**
> Let us share a sign of Christ's peace with one another.

CLOSING SONG (OPTIONAL)

Choose from #97–148 or sing additional verses of the Evening Hymn, if appropriate.

RECONCILIATION OF SEVERAL PENITENTS
with Individual Confession and Absolution

We are all in need of God's mercy because we have sinned. In the Sacrament of Penance, the priest represents Christ and the community as we ask forgiveness for our sins. One of the best ways to experience the power of that reconciliation is in communal prayer since sin always harms the community. This communal rite involves listening to the scriptures calling us to conversion, reflecting on our lives in response to that word of God, and helping each other in common prayer. After everyone has had an opportunity to individually confess and receive absolution, everyone joins in praise of God's everlasting love and mercy.

INTRODUCTORY RITES

OPENING SONG

Choose an appropriate hymn or song from #97–148, or psalm from #53–96.

GREETING

Grace, mercy, and peace be with you from God the Father and Christ Jesus our Savior.
And also with you.

OPENING PRAYER

Brothers and sisters, God calls us to conversion;
let us therefore ask for the grace of sincere repentance.

After silent prayer, the presider continues:
Lord, hear the prayers of those who call on you,
forgive the sins of those who confess to you,
and in your merciful love, give us your pardon and your peace.
We ask this through Christ, our Lord.
Amen.

CELEBRATION OF THE WORD OF GOD

FIRST READINGS

Choose one or more passages from scripture. If there are several readings, a psalm or period of silence should come between them. If there is only one reading, it should be from the gospel.

After each reading the lector says,

> The word of the Lord.
> **Thanks be to God.**

RESPONSORIAL PSALM

Choose a psalm from #53–92. Psalm 51 (#66) is commonly used for reconciliation. A hymn or song from #168–213 may also be appropriate.

GOSPEL ACCLAMATION

Choose an Alleluia or Lenten Gospel Acclamation from Mass Settings & Ritual Music #20–52.

GOSPEL

> The Lord be with you.
> **And also with you.**
> A reading from the holy gospel according to N.
> **Glory to you, Lord.**
>
> *After the reading the priest or deacon says,*
> The gospel of the Lord.
> **Praise to you, Lord Jesus Christ.**

HOMILY

EXAMINATION OF CONSCIENCE

A period of time may be spent in making an examination of conscience and in arousing true sorrow for sins. The priest or another minister may help the faithful by reading brief statements or reciting a kind of litany, taking into consideration the needs, ages and gifts of those in attendance.

RITE OF RECONCILIATION

GENERAL CONFESSION OF SINS

All kneel and join in saying the following or a similar confession of sins:

> I confess to almighty God, and you my brothers and sisters,
> that I have sinned through my own fault
> in my thoughts and in my words,
> in what I have done, and in what I have failed to do;
> and I ask blessed Mary, ever virgin,
> all the angels and saints, and you, my brothers and sisters,
> to pray for me to the Lord our God.

All stand and join in the following or a similar litany asking for God's mercy:

> Almighty God, **give us the grace to be truly sorry for our sins.**
> Merciful God, **forgive us as we admit our sins.**
> Awesome God, **free us from the debt of our sins.**
> Compassionate God, **heal our troubled hearts.**
> Faithful God, **revive our weary spirits.**
> Loving God, **give us pardon and peace.**
>
> Now, let us pray in the words that Jesus taught us, asking God to forgive us
> as we forgive others.
> **Our Father...**
> **for the kingdom, the power, and the glory are yours, now and forever.**
> **Amen.**

The priest concludes:

> Lord, draw near to your people,
> who, in the presence of your Church, confess that they are sinners.
> Through the ministry of the Church free them from all sin,
> so that renewed in spirit, they may give you thankful praise.
> We ask this through Christ our Lord.
> **Amen.**

INDIVIDUAL CONFESSION AND ABSOLUTION

Penitents now go to the priests for individual confession. They receive and accept a fitting act of satisfaction (penance), suitable counsel, and then, absolution. Everything else customary in individual confession is omitted.

PROCLAMATION OF PRAISE FOR GOD'S MERCY

When individual confessions have concluded, the presider invites all to thank God, by their good works, for the grace of repentance. It is fitting to pray a spontaneous or composed litany of thanks, or to sing a psalm, song, or canticle at this time. Choose from #53–96, #97–148, or #168–213.

CONCLUDING PRAYER OF THANKSGIVING

> All holy and living God,
> you have shown us your mercy and made us a new creation.
> Make us living signs of your love for the whole world to see.
> We ask this through Christ our Lord.
> **Amen.**

CONCLUDING RITE

BLESSING

> May the Lord guide your hearts in the way of his love.
> **Amen.**
> May God give you strength and patience to walk in the light and resist temptation.
> **Amen.**
> May Almighty God bless you, the Father, and the Son, + and the Holy Spirit.
> **Amen.**

DISMISSAL

> Go in peace to walk in the light of God's merciful love.
> **Thanks be to God.**

CLOSING SONG

Choose a final song or hymn from #97–148, if appropriate.

PSALMS, PRAYERS & CANTICLES

COMMON RESPONSORIAL PSALMS

This is a listing of the 22 Common Responsorial Psalms and the Spirit & Song titles that correspond to each of those liturgical seasons.

Psalm 25	Advent	To You, O God, I Lift Up My Soul.	# 60
Psalm 85	Advent	Lord, Let Us See Your Kindness	71
Psalm 98	Christmas	All the Ends of the Earth	75
Psalm 72	Epiphany	Lord, Every Nation	70
Psalm 51	Lent	Be Merciful, O Lord	66
Psalm 91	Lent	Be With Me	72
Psalm 130	Lent	With the Lord	86
Psalm 22	Holy Week	My God, My God	58
Psalm 136	Easter Vigil	God's Love Is Everlasting	87
Psalm 118	Easter	Let Us Rejoice and Be Glad.	81
		This Is the Day	82
Psalm 66	Easter	Let All the Earth	69
Psalm 47	Ascension	Shouts of Joy	65
		All People, Clap Your Hands	64
Psalm 104	Pentecost	Envía Tu Espíritu	78
		Send Out Your Spirit	79
Psalm 19	Ordinary	Your Words Are Spirit and Life	56
Psalm 27	Ordinary	The Lord Is My Light	61
Psalm 34	Ordinary	Taste and See	62
		O Taste and See	159
Psalm 63	Ordinary	My Soul Is Thirsting	68
Psalm 95	Ordinary	If Today	74
Psalm 100	Ordinary	We Are God's People	76
Psalm 103	Ordinary	The Lord Is Kind and Merciful	77
Psalm 122	Ordinary	I Rejoiced	84
		Qué Alegría/I Rejoiced	85
Psalm 145	Ordinary	I Will Lift Up Your Name	91

Keep Me Safe, O God
Psalm 16

53

Psalm 16:5, 8–11

Jesse Manibusan

Psalms, Prayers & Canticles

54

Path of Life
Psalm 16

Psalm 16:1–2, 5, 7–9, 11

Trevor Thomson

INTRO *Calypso (♩ = ca. 112)*

G   Am   G

REFRAIN

Melody

Lord,— you will show— us the path of life, show us the path—

Harmony

— of life. Lord,— you will show— us the path

of life, show us the path— of life.

to Verses

Last time

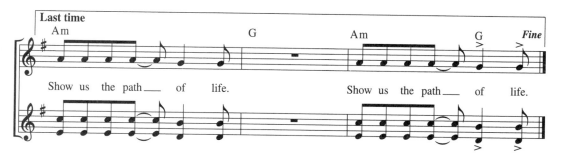

Show us the path ___ of life. Show us the path ___ of life.

VERSES

1. Keep me, ___ O God, ___ for in you ___ I ___ take ref - uge; ___
2. My heart ___ is glad, ___ my ___ soul ___ re - joic - es. ___
3. I set ___ the Lord ___ ev - er ___ be - fore ___ me. ___
4. Pro - tect ___ me, God, ___ for ___ you ___ are ___ my ref - uge. ___
5. I bless ___ you, God, ___ for ___ you ___ are ___ my teach - er. ___
6. My heart ___ is glad, ___ my ___ bod - y thrills ___ with life. ___

1. I ___ say ___ to you, "My ___ God are you." ___
2. You ___ it is ___ who holds ___ fast my lot. ___
3. He's at my ___ right hand; ___ I shall not be dis - turbed. ___
4. I ___ praise ___ you, God, ___ for you ___ are my strength. ___
5. E - ven ___ at night ___ you ___ guide my heart. ___
6. My ___ whole ___ be - ing ___ rests ___ safe in you. ___

55 I Love You, Lord/Te Amo, Señor
Psalm 18

Based on Psalm 18

Julie and Tim Smith

REFRAIN/ESTRIBILLO (♩ = ca. 102)

I love you, Lord,_____ my rock, my de-liv-er-er._____ I

love you, Lord,_____ my strength and my song._____ Te a-mo, Se-ñor,

_____ mi ro-ca y li-be-ra-dor._____ Te a-mo, Se-ñor,

1-4 / to Verses: _____ mi fuer-za y can-ción._____

Final: - ción._____ *Fine*

VERSE/ESTROFA 1

1. In my dis-tress_____ I call un-to Yah-weh,_____

1. and to my God_____ I cry. Lord, you

1. hear me; you know my voice._____ *D.C.*

Play first eight measures as an Intro.

VERSE/ESTROFA 2

2. Ví - va el Se - ñor,_____ ben - di - ta se - a mi ro - ca._____

2. Tú dis - te gran vic - to - ri - a a tu rey tú

2. dis - te mi - se - ri - cor - dia a tu un - gi - do._____

VERSE/ESTROFA 3

3. Bles - sed be my rock,_____ ex - tolled be my Sav - ior,_____

3. who gave great vic - to - ry_____ to me and showed

3. kind - ness to your a - noint - ed._____

VERSE/ESTROFA 4

4. In - vo - co al Se - ñor_____ de mi al - a - ban - za_____

4. y que - do li - bre de mis__ en - e - mi - gos,___ mi

4. fuer - za sal - va - do - ra, mi bal - u - ar - te._____

Prayer for Peace

This is an inter-faith prayer service. Adapt as needed for the faiths represented.

GATHERING

> We gather in the name of peace.
> **Let there be true peace on earth.**

Each group, denomination, faith, or culture lights a candle and brings it forward.
(Pause in silence to reverence the Holy One.)

> We gather, each from our own tradition, but all with a common purpose—
> to pray for peace and an end to all violence:
> **among cultures and between nations;**
> **among faiths and between denominations;**
> **among families and between persons.**
> **We pray for an end to all acts of violence and hatred.**

READINGS

Several passages from the Bible and other holy books may be read at this time.
Consider Isaiah 55:6–13; Psalm 29; Matthew 5:1–12; and 2 Corinthians 13:11–12.

RESPONSE

> Source of Human Life,
> you are the foundation of peace, among every race and people;
> among every city, village, tribe, and nation.
> **Break the chains of prejudice and hatred.**
> **Teach us to put aside war and injustice.**
> **Draw us to live in peace and harmony.**
> **Show us how to honor our differences.**

A single, larger candle is lit. All other candles are extinguished.

SENDING FORTH

> We pray in the words of Francis of Assisi:
> make me an instrument of your peace;
> **where there is hatred, let me sow love;**
> **where there is injury, pardon;**
> **where there is doubt, faith;**
> **where there is despair, hope;**
> **where there is darkness, light;**
> **where there is sadness, joy.**
> For it is in giving that we receive;
> in pardoning that we are pardoned;
> and in dying that we are born to life.

All now extend a sign of peace with one another.

Your Words Are Spirit and Life
Psalm 19

56

Based on Psalm 19:8–11

Bernadette Farrell

57

I Will Praise You, Lord
Psalm 22

Psalm 22:23, 26–27, 31–32

Julie and Tim Smith

2-3 Dmaj7/E E7 *to Verses* | **Final** Dmaj7/E E7 A *Fine*

peo - ple.___ peo - ple.___ I will___ praise___ you, Lord.

VERSES

A/E   D/E

1. My vows I___ will make be - fore the ones who___ fear___
2. Pro - claim to___ a peo - ple who are yet to___ be

C#m/E

1. ___ the Lord. The poor shall___ eat___ and have their
2. born___ the jus - tice,___ the faith - ful - ness of

D/E   A/E

1. fill.___ ⁋ They will___ serve the Lord,___
2. God.___ My soul shall___ live for the Lord, my

D/E   C#m/E

1. all who___ bless___ the Lord, hearts filled___ with
2. chil - dren___ will serve the Lord, faith - ful___ in

D/E   D E *D.S.*

1. joy that lasts for - ev - er.___
2. ev - 'ry gen - er - a - tion.___

58 My God, My God
Psalm 22

Psalm 22:8–9, 17–20, 23–24

Timothy R. Smith

REFRAIN *Moderato (♩ = 88-92)*

Capo 3: **(Bm)** ... **(F♯m/B)** **(Gmaj7/B)** **(F♯m/B)**

Melody: My God, my God, why have you a-

Harmony

(Em7/B) Gm7/D | **1** **(Bm)** Dm *D.C.* | **2-5** **(Bm)** Dm *to Verses* | **Final** **(Bm)** Dm *Fine*

ban - doned me?

VERSE 1

(F♯m) Am | **(Gsus2)** B♭sus2 | **(F♯m)** Am

1. All who see me scoff; they mock me with part - ed

(Gsus2) B♭sus2 | **(Bm)** Dm | **(F♯m/A)** Am/C

1. lips, they wag their heads: "He re - lied on the Lord, let him de -

(Gsus2) B♭sus2 | **(D/F♯)** F/A | **(Em7)** Gm7 | **(F♯m/B)** Am/D **(Bm)** Dm *D.C.*

1. liv - er him. ___ let him res - cue him, if he loves him."

VERSE 2

(F♯m) Am | **(Gsus2)** B♭sus2 | **(Bm)** Dm

2. In - deed man - y dogs sur - round ___ me, a

Play Refrain as an Intro.

Psalms, Prayers & Canticles

59 Shepherd Me, O God
Psalm 23

Based on Psalm 23

Marty Haugen

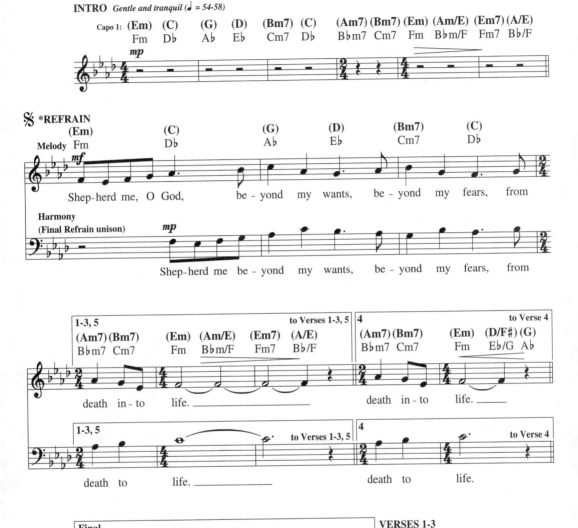

*Final Refrain softer and a bit slower.

VERSE 4

VERSE 5

60 To You, O God, I Lift Up My Soul
Psalm 25

Based on Psalm 25:1, 4–5, 8–9, 10, 14

Bob Hurd
Harmony by Craig Kingsbury

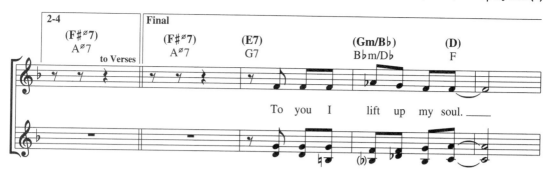

VERSES

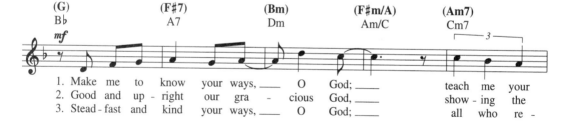

1. Make me to know your ways, ___ O God; ___ teach me your
2. Good and up-right our gra - cious God, ___ show-ing the
3. Stead-fast and kind your ways, ___ O God; ___ all who re -

1. paths, guide me. You are my sav-ior. _____
2. way, guid-ing the hum-ble to jus-tice. _____
3. vere your cov-e-nant know your friend-ship. _____

61

The Lord Is My Light
Psalm 27

Based on Psalm 27

Christopher Walker

1. The Lord is my light, my help, my sal-va-tion. Why should I fear? With God I fear no one. God pro-tects me all my life. With the Lord what should I dread?

2. There is one thing I ask of the Lord that I long for: all of my days with God to be dwell-ing, gaz-ing with awe at the beau-ty of God, and in won-der look on God's house.

3. I know I will live to see the Lord's good-ness, now, in this life I'm sure I will see it. Trust in the Lord, be strong and be brave; wait in hope for God, our sal-va-tion.

REFRAIN

The Lord is my light, the Lord is my help, the __ Lord is

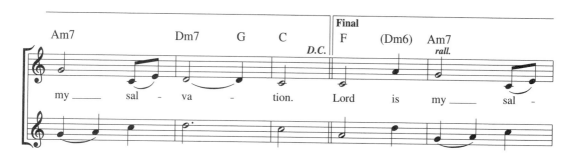

my __ sal - va - tion. Lord is my __ sal -

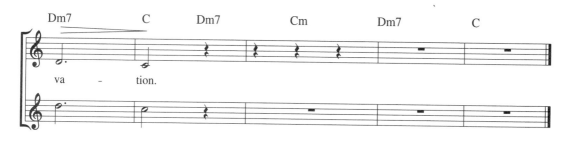

va - tion.

62

Taste and See
Psalm 34

Psalm 34:2–4, 9; 136:5–6;
Luke 1:52

Bob Hurd
Harmony by Craig Kingsbury

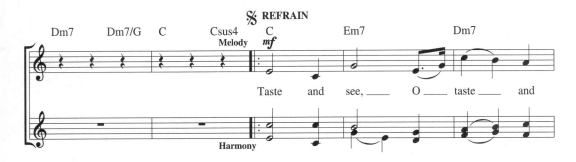

Taste and see, __ O __ taste __ and

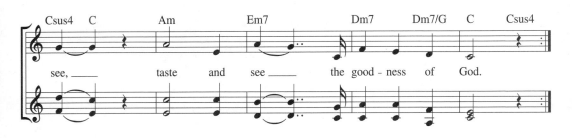

see, __ taste and see __ the good-ness of God.

VERSES 1, 2

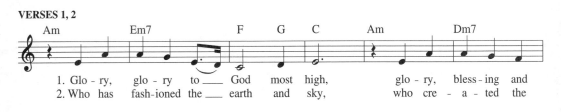

1. Glo - ry, glo - ry to __ God most high, glo - ry, bless - ing and
2. Who has fash-ioned the __ earth and sky, who cre - a - ted the

1. praise. _____ With one voice, O peo - ple, re - joice in our
2. deep, _____ who ex - alts the low - ly and sets cap - tives

Psalms, Prayers & Canticles

63 The Cry of the Poor
Psalm 34

Based on Psalm 34:2–3, 17–19, 23

John Foley, S.J.

INTRO *Moderate tempo* ($\bullet$ = 66)   **REFRAIN**

Capo 2: (Em)   (D)   (Bm)   (Em)

mp (a tempo)

The Lord hears the cry of the poor.

VERSES *Slightly faster* ($\bullet$ = 76)

(C)   (D)   (Em)   (C)   (D)

Fine mf

Bless - ed be the Lord. _____

1. I will bless the Lord at all
2. Let the low - ly hear and be
3. Ev - 'ry spir - it crushed, God will
4. We pro - claim your great - ness, O

(Em)   (C)   (G)   (Am)   (Bm)   (Bm7)

1. times, _____ with praise ev - er in my mouth. _____
2. glad: _____ the Lord lis - tens to their pleas; _____
3. save; _____ will be ran - som for their lives; _____
4. God, _____ your praise ev - er in our mouth; _____

(F)   (B)   (Em)   (C)

1. Let my soul glo - ry in the Lord, _____ who will
2. and to hearts bro - ken, God is near, _____ who will
3. will be safe shel - ter for their fears, _____ and will
4. ev - 'ry face bright - ened in your light, _____ for you

(Am7)   (Bm)   (Em)

rit.   *D.S.*

1-4. hear the cry of the poor. _____

Prayer for World Youth Day

Divide the speaking parts between two readers, two sides, or men and women, as appropriate.

1   Two thousand years have passed since you walked among us, O Lord.
The fleeting days of our youth are spent in the search
for happiness that truly fills the heart.

2   O Lord Jesus, help us to see and to believe
that this world, so spoiled by injustice, conflict and emptiness,
can be born to new life, only in you.

All   **Jesus Christ, Son of God, we are your brothers and sisters.
We love you, we follow you!**

1   The Pope calls us to the Jubilee of your Incarnation, O Lord.
We answer his call with eagerness and hope,
anxious to find you, to know you and to know we are brothers and sisters
in your Church.

2   Lord Jesus, free our hearts of fear and sin,
renew them through the experience of love and forgiveness,
so we may put our lives at the service of the poor.

All   **Jesus Christ, Son of God, we are your brothers and sisters.
We love you, we follow you!**

1   From every corner of the earth we turn our steps to Rome, O Lord.
May the memory of Peter, Paul and many other witnesses to the Faith
confirm for us the message of your Gospel.

2   Change us, Lord Jesus. Make us, like Mary, open with confidence
to welcome the Word of truth and life
which your Church entrusts to us for the Third Millennium.

All   **Make us your witnesses for those who have yet to meet you.
Jesus Christ, Son of God, we are your brothers and sisters.
We love you, we follow you!**

*—Prayer for the 15th World Youth Day.
(Text modified for group recitation.)*

64 All People, Clap Your Hands
Psalm 47

Psalm 47: 1–2, 5–8
Verses 2 & 4 by Timothy R. Smith

Timothy R. Smith

65

Shouts of Joy
Psalm 47

Psalm 47:2–3, 6–9

Ken Canedo

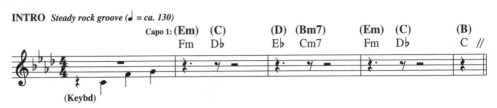

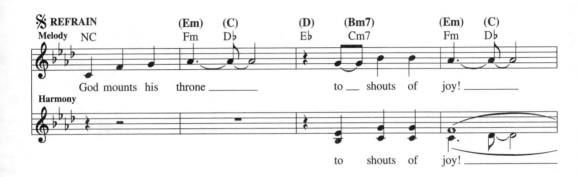

God mounts his throne _____ to __ shouts of joy! _____

(Harmony) to shouts of joy! _____

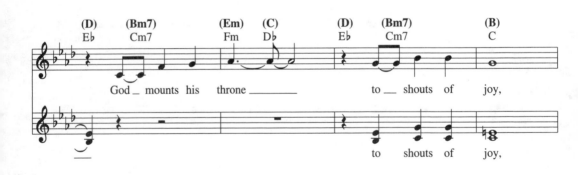

God __ mounts his throne _____ to __ shouts of joy,

to shouts of joy,

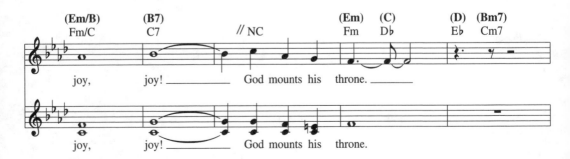

joy, joy! _____ God mounts his throne. _____

joy, joy! _____ God mounts his throne.

VERSES

1. All you peo - ple, clap your hands, __ and shout to God __ with
2. For the Lord as - cends the throne; __ the trum - pet sounds __ with
3. Let us now ac - claim our God __ as rul - er of __ the

1. joy, for the awe - some Lord now rules the earth. _____
2. joy! Come and join __ the song of praise to God. _____
3. world! Let the na - tions know God's reign is here. _____

66 Be Merciful, O Lord
Psalm 51

Psalm 51:3–4, 12–13, 17

Steve Angrisano

Psalms, Prayers & Canticles

67 The Lord Upholds My Life
Psalm 54

Psalm 54:1, 2, 4–7

Jeffrey Roscoe

VERSE 2

2. Be my faith-ful friend, __ O Lord! _____ Pro-tect me from __ my en-

2. e-mies, ___ and from their e-vil deeds. _____ Give me __ your _____ hand, and

2. I will stand be - fore them, O Lord. _____

VERSE 3

3. Yes, I will bring a gift, _____ a sac-ri-fice __ to you! __ And all those who

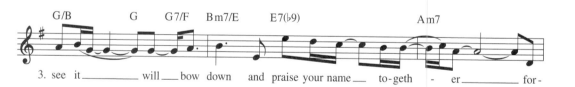

3. see it _____ will __ bow down and praise your name __ to-geth - er _____ for-

3. ev - er, _____ for it is good. _____

My Soul Is Thirsting / As Morning Breaks
Psalm 63

Psalm 63:2–9

Steve Angrisano

VERSES 1,2

1. O____ God, you are____ my God,____ and____ I will al -
2. Through the day you walk____ with me;____ all the night your love____

1. - ways praise_____ you. In the shad - ow of____ your wings____
2. ___ sur - rounds_____ me. To the glo - ry of____ your name____

1. ___ I cling____ to____ you____ and you hold me high.
2. ___ I lift____ my____ hands,____ I sing your praise.

INTERLUDE

(Keybd)

(to Verse 3)

VERSE 3

3. I will nev - er be____ a - fraid,____ for I will not be____ a - ban - doned. E - ven

3. when the road____ grows long____ and wea - ry your love will res - cue____ me.

69 Let All the Earth
Psalm 66

Psalm 66:1–5, 16

Steve Angrisano and Tom Tomaszek

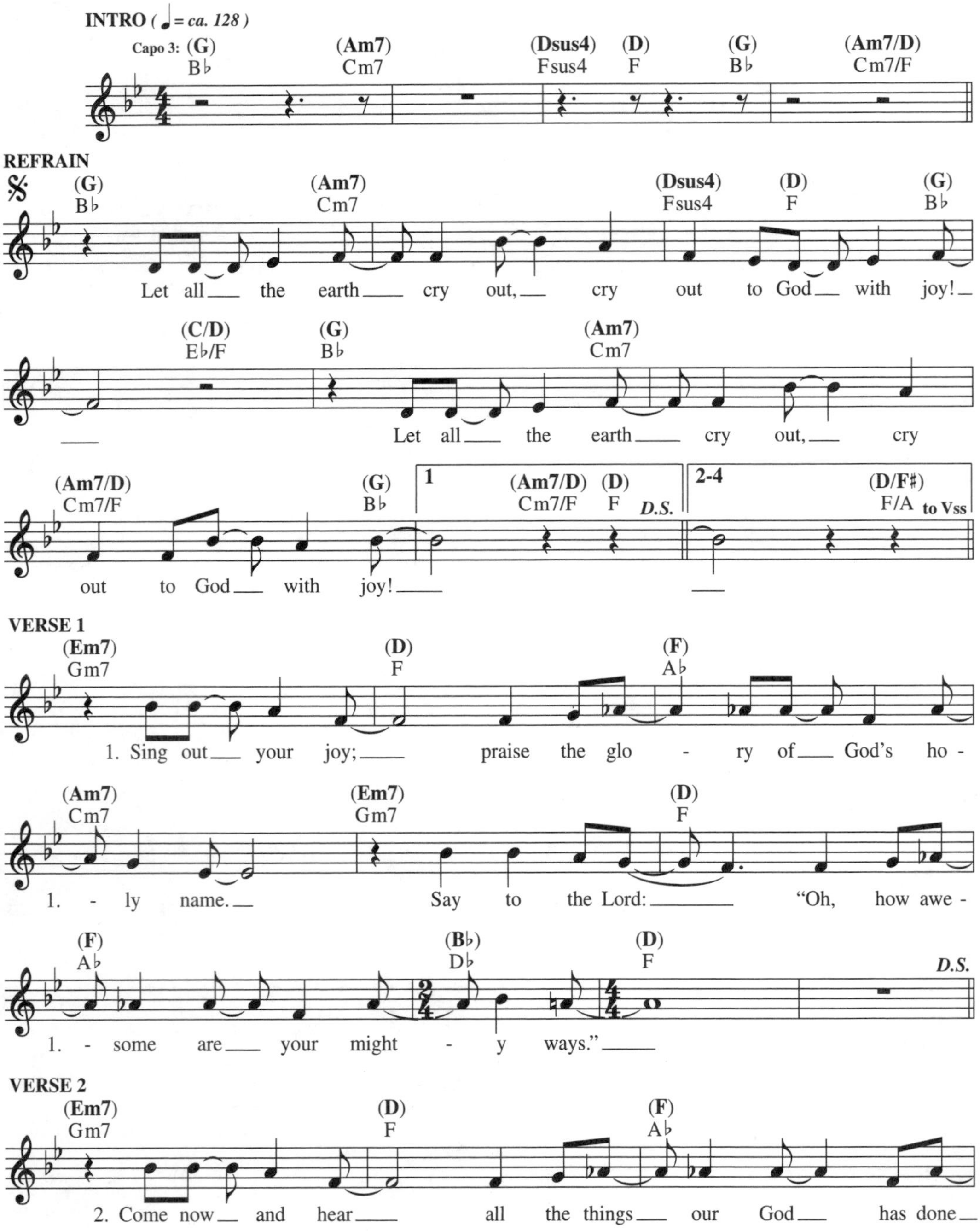

INTRO (♩ = ca. 128)

REFRAIN

Let all the earth cry out, cry out to God with joy!

Let all the earth cry out, cry

out to God with joy!

VERSE 1

1. Sing out your joy; praise the glo - ry of God's ho -

1. - ly name. Say to the Lord: "Oh, how awe -

1. - some are your might - y ways."

VERSE 2

2. Come now and hear all the things our God has done

Psalms, Prayers & Canticles

70 Lord, Every Nation
Psalm 72

Psalm 72:1–2, 7–8, 10–13

Jesse Manibusan

VERSE 2

VERSE 3

71

Lord, Let Us See Your Kindness
Psalm 85

Psalm 85

Paul Hillebrand

For an Intro, play the Refrain with repeat, using first ending twice.

VERSE 2

2. Kind - ness ___ and truth shall meet, jus - tice and peace shall kiss;

2. truth shall spring ___ out of _____ the earth, and jus - tice shall

2. look down from heav - en.

VERSE 3 (Instrumental)

72

Be With Me
Psalm 91

Based on Psalm 91:1–2, 10–11, 12, 14–15

Bob Hurd

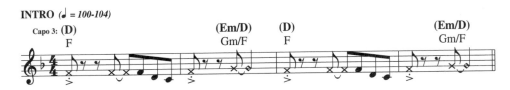

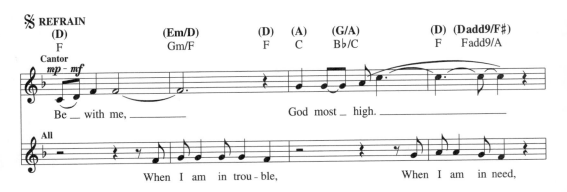

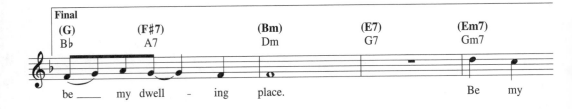

VERSES

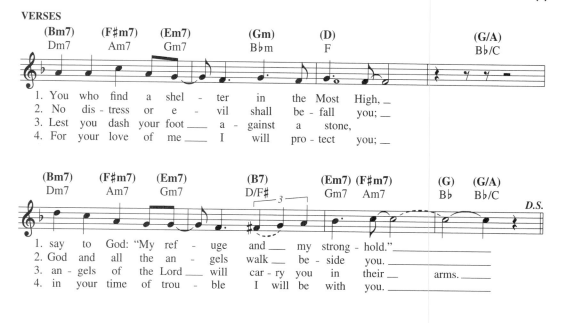

1. You who find a shel - ter in the Most High, _
2. No dis - tress or e - vil shall be - fall you; _
3. Lest you dash your foot ___ a - gainst a stone,
4. For your love of me ___ I will pro - tect you; _

1. say to God: "My ref - uge and ___ my strong - hold."_____
2. God and all the an - gels walk ___ be - side you._____
3. an - gels of the Lord ___ will car - ry you in their ___ arms._____
4. in your time of trou - ble I will be with you._____

Prayer of Surrender

Jesus, O Sacred Heart of Love,
You are my happiness,
    my comfort,
    my joy.
You charmed me in my tender youth.
You know my deepest desires.
You are my companion for life.

Heart of Jesus,
may I lose myself in you.
Guide my life.
Let your will be done in me.

Jesus, O Sacred Heart of Love,
I surrender all.

*—Adapted from a Prayer to the Sacred Heart
attributed to St. Thérèse of Lisieux*

73 Come, Worship the Lord
Psalm 95

Based on Psalm 95:1–7

John Michael Talbot

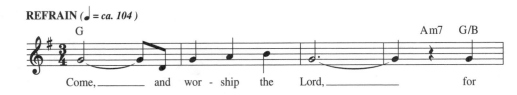

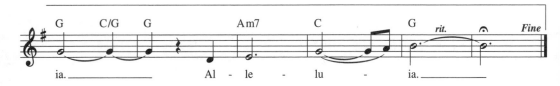

1. joy_____ to the rock who saves us. Let us
3. knee be-fore the Lord our mak - er. For

1. come with thanks - giv - ing, and sing joy - ful
3. we are his peo - ple, we are the

D   C/D   G/D   D   *D.C.*

1. songs to the Lord._____ So
3. flock that he____ shep - herds._____

VERSE 2

G

2. The Lord is God, the might - y God, the great king o'er

C/G   G

2. all oth - er gods._____ He holds in his hands the

A

2. depths of the earth and the high - est moun - tains as well.

Asus4   A   Am

2. He made the sea, it be - longs now to him; the dry land, __

D   C/D   G/D   D   *D.C.*

2. too, was formed by his hand._____

74

If Today
Psalm 95

Psalm 95:1–2, 7–9

Trevor Thomson

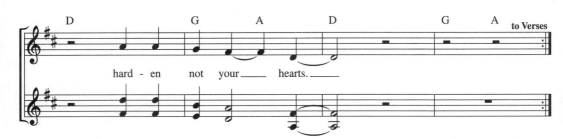

VERSE 1

VERSE 2

75 All the Ends of the Earth
Psalm 98

Based on Psalm 98

Bobby Fisher

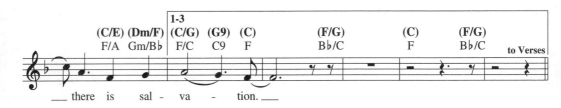

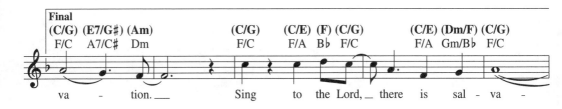

Psalms, Prayers & Canticles

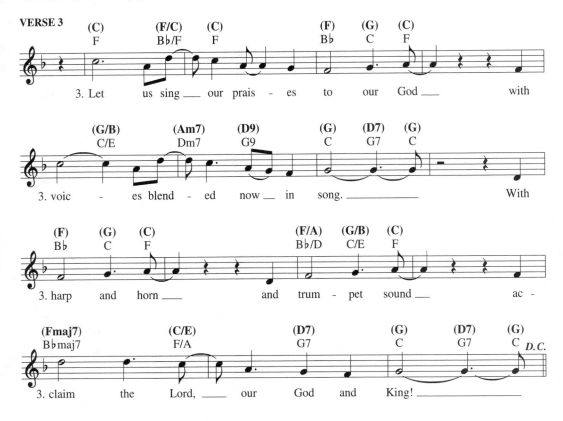

VERSE 3

3. Let us sing ___ our prais - es to our God ___ with

3. voic - es blend - ed now ___ in song. ___ With

3. harp and horn ___ and trum - pet sound ___ ac -

3. claim the Lord, ___ our God and King! ___

Seeker's Prayer

Dear God,
I am searching for you.
I've been to your house and I've *prayed* at times.
I've listened to other people talk about you,
but I'm not sure I really *know* you.
Please don't be offended by my questions, or my doubts.
I don't mean to upset you or anyone else (even though they are!)
I just want to meet you on my own.
So, here I am.

Prayer before a Religious Education Session

Our help is in the name of the Lord.
Who made heaven and earth.
(All make the Sign of the Cross.)
Glory be to the Father, and to the Son, and to the Holy Spirit,
as it was in the beginning, is now, and will be forever. Amen.

Today we will be discussing... *(Say a few brief words about the topics or aspect of the faith that will form the session.)*... and so we pray:

Almighty God and Source of all Wisdom,
bless those who seek to know you and understand your Word.
Bless our time of study and reflection. Bless our conversation.
May your Holy Spirit guide us to wonder and awe in your goodness.
We want to know you and discover our place in your Church.
We want to tell the stories of your presence in our lives.
Make us true disciples and witnesses of your love.
Teach us, Master. You are our Way, our Truth, and Life.
We make this prayer through Christ, our Teacher and Savior.
Amen.

God's Response

Dear Seeker,
I have loved you forever.
Before you were born,
    I knew you, named you, and cared for you.
I made you to shine as a special star in my heavens.
I will never abandon you.
Even when it seems to you that I cannot be near,
I am here.

76

We Are God's People
Psalm 100

Psalm 100:1–3, 5

Jeffrey Roscoe

VERSE 2

77 The Lord Is Kind and Merciful
Psalm 103

Rick Modlin
Harmony by Craig Kingsbury

Psalm 103:1–4, 8, 10, 12–13

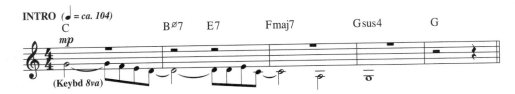

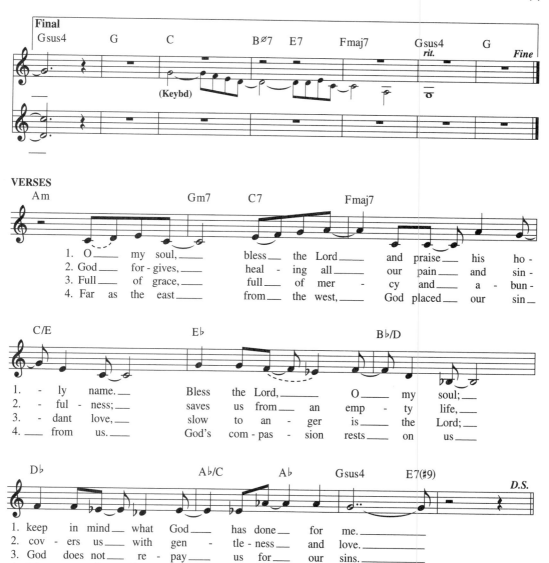

Final

Gsus4   G   C   Bø7   E7   Fmaj7   Gsus4   G
                                               rit.   *Fine*

(Keybd)

VERSES

Am   Gm7   C7   Fmaj7

1. O___ my soul,___ bless___ the Lord___ and praise___ his ho-
2. God___ for-gives,___ heal - ing all___ our pain___ and sin-
3. Full___ of grace,___ full___ of mer - cy and___ a - bun-
4. Far as the east___ from___ the west,___ God placed___ our sin

C/E   Eb   Bb/D

1. - ly name.___ Bless the Lord,___ O___ my soul;___
2. - ful - ness;___ saves us from___ an emp - ty life,___
3. - dant love,___ slow to an - ger is___ the Lord;___
4. ___ from us.___ God's com - pas - sion rests___ on us___

Db   Ab/C   Ab   Gsus4   E7(#9)
                                              D.S.

1. keep in mind___ what God___ has done___ for me.___
2. cov - ers us___ with gen - tle - ness___ and love.___
3. God does not___ re - pay___ us for___ our sins.___
4. like a fa - ther's mer - cy for___ his own.___

78

Envía Tu Espíritu
Psalm 104

Psalm 104:30, *Veni Sancte Spiritus*
Adapted by Bob Hurd

Bob Hurd

*Send out your Spirit, and renew the face of the earth.

VERSES

1. Spir - it of ___ the liv - ing God, ___ burn in our hearts, ___
2. Wind of prom - ise, wind ___ of change, ___ friend of the poor, ___
3. Breath of life ___ and ho - li - ness, ___ heal ev - 'ry wound, ___

1. ___ and make us a peo - ple of hope ___
2. ___ em - pow - er your peo - ple to make ___
3. ___ and lead us be - yond ___ ev - 'ry sin ___

1. ___ and com - pas - sion. ___
2. ___ peace and jus - tice. ___
3. ___ that di - vides ___ us ___

En -

79

Send Out Your Spirit
Psalm 104

Based on Psalm 104

Jesse Manibusan

INTRO (♩ = ca. 112)

REFRAIN

O God, send out your Spir-it; re-new the face of the earth. O God, send out your Spir-it;

1,6 re-new the face of the earth.

2-5, Final face of the earth. *to Verses Fine*

VERSE 1

1. We bless you, O God, for you are so great. Your Spir-it un-cov-ers hid-den

1. beau-ty and grace. Though times we de-ny all the pain and the tears, your

1. Spir-it em-pow-ers us and soon we face our fear. *D.S.*

VERSE 2

2. Ev-'ry prayer we pray, sa-cred word, sa-cred rite, is for the

Psalms, Prayers & Canticles

Thank God for He Is Good

Psalm 118

Psalm 118:1–4, 21–24

Jeffrey Roscoe

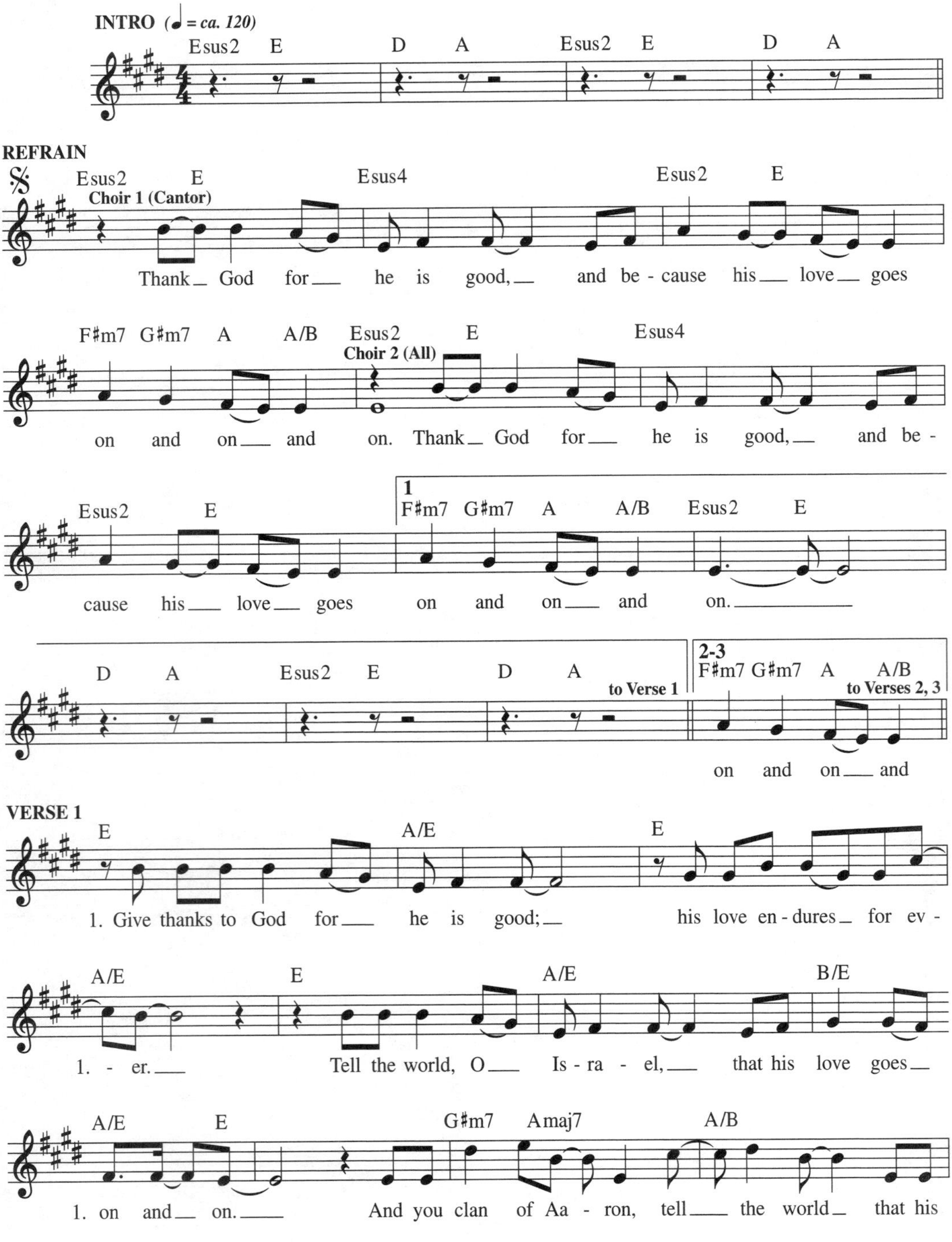

INTRO (♩ = ca. 120)
Esus2 E D A Esus2 E D A
REFRAIN
Esus2 E Esus4 Esus2 E
Choir 1 (Cantor)
Thank God for he is good, and be - cause his love goes
F#m7 G#m7 A A/B Esus2 E Esus4
Choir 2 (All)
on and on and on. Thank God for he is good, and be -
Esus2 E
cause his love goes
1
F#m7 G#m7 A A/B Esus2 E
on and on and on.
D A Esus2 E D A
to Verse 1
2-3
F#m7 G#m7 A A/B
to Verses 2, 3
on and on and
VERSE 1
E A/E E
1. Give thanks to God for he is good; his love en - dures for ev -
A/E E A/E B/E
1. - er. Tell the world, O Is - ra - el, that his love goes
A/E E G#m7 Amaj7 A/B
1. on and on. And you clan of Aa - ron, tell the world that his

Psalms, Prayers & Canticles

FINAL REFRAIN

Let Us Rejoice and Be Glad
Psalm 118

81

Psalm 118:1, 4, 13–15, 22–24

Tom Tomaszek

Psalms, Prayers & Canticles

82

This Is the Day
Psalm 118

Psalm 118

Bobby Fisher

1. Let us re-joice ___ and be glad. _____

VERSE 2

2. Give thanks to the Lord! ___ Our God is ___ good,

2. whose love en-dures ___ for - ev - er.

2. Let all the chil - dren of Is - rael ___ say:

2. God's love en-dures ___ for - ev - er. ___

VERSE 3

3. The right hand of God ___ has struck with ___ pow'r. The

3. right hand of God ___ is ex - alt - ed.

3. I shall not die, ___ but I shall ___ live and pro-claim ___

3. ___ the works _____ of the Lord! ___

VERSE 4

4. The stone which the build — ers re - ject - ed ___

4. ___ has be - come the foun-da - tion of our house!

4. By ___ the Lord has this been ___ done.

4. How won - der - ful ___ to be - hold! _____

Prayer before a Mission or Service Trip

GATHERING

Sing a song, hymn, or psalm antiphon if appropriate.

Let us ask God to bless us as we prepare for…*(name the event).*
God, our Companion on this pilgrimage of service,
watch over us as we leave our homes and places of comfort
so that we might serve others in your name.
Open our hearts and calm our fears,
so that we can be joyful messengers of your love and mercy,
and see you clearly in the faces of those we will serve.
We make this prayer in Jesus' name.
Amen.

READINGS

Select one or more passages from the Bible to read and reflect on at this time.
Consider Isaiah 61:1–11; Matthew 9:35–10:1; Luke 9:1–8; and John 20:19–22.
After each reading the lector says,

The word of the Lord.
Thanks be to God.

If there is a theme or pilgrim song, this is an appropriate time to sing or play it.

RESPONSE

Bring forward some reminder or symbol of the place or people who will be served.

Good and gracious God,
thank you for the opportunity to work in your vineyard.
May this *(refer to the symbol)* remind us of the tasks before us.
May our service yield a rich harvest, we pray to the Lord,
Lord, hear our prayer.

Add any additional spontaneous or composed prayers followed by the Lord's Prayer.

SENDING FORTH

The symbol is given to someone from the community who will remain home.

Keep this *(refer to the symbol)* as a reminder of our need for your support.
Pray for us as we will pray for you.
(All make the Sign of the Cross.)
Glory be to the Father, and to the Son, and to the Holy Spirit,
as it was in the beginning, is now, and will be forever. Amen.

All exchange a sign of peace. Sing a song of praise or journey if appropriate.

Psalms, Prayers & Canticles

83

I Will Lift Up My Eyes
Psalm 121

Based on Psalm 121

Cyprian Consiglio

84

I Rejoiced
Psalm 122

Psalm 122:1–4, 8–9

Trevor Thomson

let us go to the house of the Lord.

VERSES

1. I re - joiced when they said to me:
2. Strong - ly built is Je - ru - sa - lem,
3. For the love of friends and fam - 'ly,

1. "Let us go to the house of the Lord to - day."
2. strong - ly built with u - ni - ty and love.
3. may the peace of God be with you al - ways.

1. And now we stand with - in your gates;
2. And it is there that the tribes go up,
3. For the love of God's house,

1. my heart is glad and I will sing with joy.
2. go up to the moun - tain of our God.
3. I will pray for you, will pray for your good.

85

Qué Alegría/I Rejoiced
Psalm 122

Psalm 122

Jaime Cortez

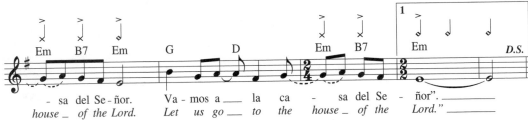

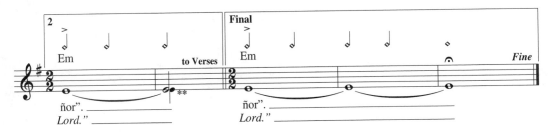

*Play Refrain once as an Intro.

The Refrain may be sung all in one language or bilingually. It is repeated in either case.

**Use cue note before Verse 4.

VERSE 1

1a. Qué a - le - grí - a cuan - do me di - je - ron: _____

1b. *I re - joiced when they said to me,* _____ *"We will*

1a. "Va - mos a la ca - sa del Se - ñor". _____ Ya - ho - ra en

1b. *go to the house of the Lord."* _____ *And now in -*

1a. tus por - ta - les _____ en - tra - mos ya, __ Je - ru - sa -

1b. *side your gates* _____ *we stand, Je - ru - sa -*

1a. lén, ____ en - tra - mos ya, __ Je - ru - sa - lén.

1b. *lem,* ____ *we stand, Je - ru - sa - lem.* _____

D.S.

VERSE 2

2a. A - llá su - ben las tri - bus de Is - ra - el a ce - le -
2b. *It is there that the tribes go up _____ to give*

2a. brar el nom - bre del Se - ñor. En e - lla es - tán los tri - bu -
2b. *thanks to the name of the Lord. _____ For it's there that the*

2a. na - les de jus - ti - cia, _____ en el pa - la - cio de Da -
2b. *thrones of judg - ment stand, _____ the thrones of the house of*

2a. vid, _____ en el pa - la - cio de Da - vid. _____
2b. *Da - vid, the thrones of the house of Da - vid.*

VERSE 3

3a. O - ren por la paz de Je - ru - sa - lén: _____ "Que
3b. *Pray _____ for the peace of Je - ru - sa - lem: _____ "Pros -*

86

With the Lord
Psalm 130

Psalm 130:1–2, 5–7

Trevor Thomson

The English translation of the refrain text from *Lectionary for Mass* © 1969, 1981, International Committee on English in the Liturgy, Inc. (ICEL). All rights reserved. Used with permission. Music and verses text © 1996, Trevor Thomson. Published by OCP Publications. All rights reserved.

Psalms, Prayers & Canticles

172

FINAL REFRAIN

Prayer in Hope of the Resurrection

A prayer for the untimely death of a young person, family member, friend or leader.

GATHERING

Sing a song or hymn as appropriate for the group gathered.

> Jesus, Healer of our hearts,
> You wept bitterly upon hearing of the death of your good friend, Lazarus, as
> we are saddened by the death of N.
> **Our hearts are heavy, Lord, and sometimes it seems just too much.**
> **But we trust in you. Be our comfort and strength.**
> **Hold us in the palm of your hand.**
> We make this prayer through Christ, our Savior and Lord.
> **Amen.**

READINGS

Select one or more passages from the Bible to read and reflect on at this time. Consider Matthew 22:23a, 29–33; John 11:17–27; 1 Corinthians 15:50–56; and Philippians 3:7–11.

After each reading the lector says,

> The word of the Lord.
> **Thanks be to God.**

If appropriate, sing a song or psalm of comfort and hope.

RESPONSE

If time permits, share some brief stories about the person who has died. Otherwise, the prayer leader should say a few words of hope in the resurrection.

> At this time we light a vigil candle in memory of N.
> *(Light the candle.)*
> **May this light be a sign of our prayers and support to all those who**
> **mourn, and a reminder of God's presence and love.**

SENDING FORTH

> Our help is in the name of the Lord.
> **Who made heaven and earth.**
> *(All make the Sign of the Cross.)*
> Glory be to the Father, and to the Son, and to the Holy Spirit,
> **as it was in the beginning, is now, and will be forever. Amen.**
> May God, who is true peace, be with you.
> **And also with you.**
> Please extend a gesture of peace and comfort to one another.

The prayer may end with a song. Consider giving a small card with a favorite saying or scripture passage of the deceased person, or a carnation to each person as they leave.

God's Love Is Everlasting
Psalm 136

Psalm 136:1–9

Tom Tomaszek

Play Refrain as an Intro.

88 Lord, Your Love Is Everlasting
Psalm 138

Psalm 138:1–3, 6, 8

Abraham Marcor

INTRO (♩ = ca. 72)

REFRAIN 1

Lord, your love is ev-er-last-ing; do not for-sake the work of your hands.

VERSE 1

1. I'll give you thanks, O Lord, with all___ my heart. For you have heard___ the

1. words of my mouth. In the pres-ence of the an-gels I will sing your

1. praise; and I will wor-ship___ at your ho-ly tem-ple.___

VERSE 2

2. Gra-cias, Se-ñor,___ yo te doy por tu bon-dad___ y tu ver-

Psalms, Prayers & Canticles

89

Behind and Before Me
Psalm 139

Based on Psalm 139

Cyprian Consiglio

INTRO (♩ = ca. 68)

Em Dadd9 Dadd9/B Em Dadd2 Em Dadd9 Dadd9/B Em Dadd9

℅ REFRAIN

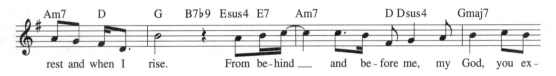

Em Dadd9 Dadd9/B Em Dadd9 Dadd9/B Em

O Lord, how you search me! __ My God, how you know me! __ You see me __ when I

Am7 D G B7♭9 Esus4 E7 Am7 D Dsus4 Gmaj7

rest and when I rise. From be-hind __ and be-fore me, my God, you ex-

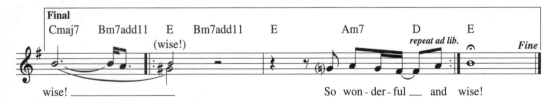

Emadd9 Am7 D | **1-3** Cmaj7 Bm7add11 E Bm7add11 E **to Verses** Em7/B

plore me; so ter-ri-ble, so won-der-ful, __ so wise!

Final
Cmaj7 Bm7add11 E Bm7add11 E Am7 D E

(wise!) *repeat ad lib.* **Fine**

wise! _____ So won-der-ful __ and wise!

VERSE 1

Am7 D G B7♭9 Esus4 Am7

1. With praise for all the won-ders I can see, how I thank you for __ the

D G B7 E7 Am7 D

1. won-der you made me. For your eyes have seen __ my ways; __ you have

Psalms, Prayers & Canticles

90 Let My Prayer Come like Incense
Psalm 141

Psalm 141:1–3, 8
Adoro te devote, ascribed to Thomas Aquinas, 1227–1274

Jeffrey Roscoe

1. Lord._____ Let my prayer come_____ like_ in - cense,_____ sweet in-
2. lips._____ To - ward you, O God,_____ my_ Lord,_____ my eyes_

1. - cense be - fore you;_ I lift up my hands_ to you_ like the eve - ning sac - ri - fice.
2. _____ are_ up-turned;_ in you,_ O Lord,_ I take_ ref - uge;_ strip me not of life._

1. _____
2. _____

Let my prayer,_____

FINAL REFRAIN: All

_ let my prayer come like in-cense be-fore_ you._ Let my prayer_____

_ come,_ come like in-cense be-fore_ you. Let my prayer

A - dó - ro te de - vó - te,

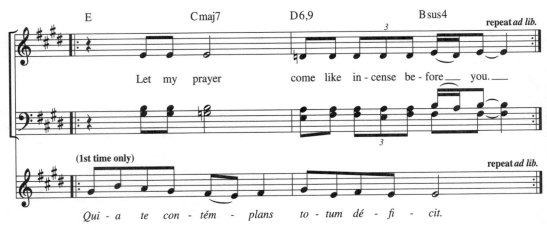

Prayer for Healing

GATHERING

Our help is in the name of the Lord.
Who made heaven and earth.
(All make the Sign of the Cross.)
Glory be to the Father, and to the Son, and to the Holy Spirit,
as it was in the beginning, is now, and will be forever. Amen.
Good and Gracious God,
we pray that *(name or names of persons who are ill)* will know the power of your
healing touch and be comforted in their time of need.
May our gathering here in prayer be a sign of your love for them,
and strengthen our faith, hope, and compassion.
We ask this through Christ our Healer and Teacher.
Amen.

READINGS

Select a passage from the Bible to read and reflect on at this time. Consider Exodus 15:26;
Psalm 30; Matthew 8:1–17; Luke 6:17–19; or Acts 4:1–12.

After the reading the lector says,

The word of the Lord.
Thanks be to God.

RESPONSE

The names of those who are physically or psychologically ill are called. If they are present,
they come forward and a member of the group places a hand on their shoulder.

We pray for God's healing upon N.
(Consider a sung response from the section of Ritual Music, #1–52, or say:)
Lord, hear our prayer and grant us your mercy.

After all names have been called, the prayer leader says:

We are confident that God hears our prayers and so we pray:
Our Father…
For the Kingdom…Amen.

SENDING FORTH

May God, who is true peace, be with you.
And also with you.
Please extend a gesture of Christ's peace to one another.

Psalms, Prayers & Canticles

91 I Will Lift Up Your Name
Psalm 145

Steve Angrisano, based on
Psalm 145:1–2, 8–11

Steve Angrisano and Tom Tomaszek

Psalms, Prayers & Canticles

92

Alaben a Dios
Psalm 150

Based on Psalm 150:1–6

Eleazar Cortés

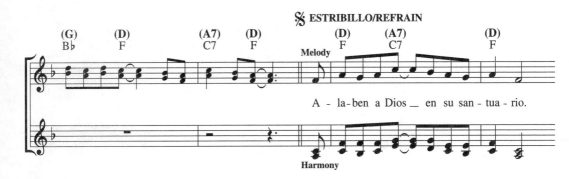

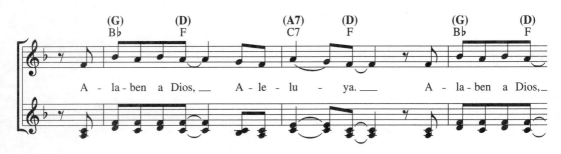

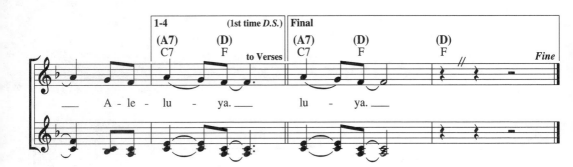

ESTROFA/VERSE 1

1. Por el fir - ma - men - to de su fuer - za y por sus gran - des ha - za -

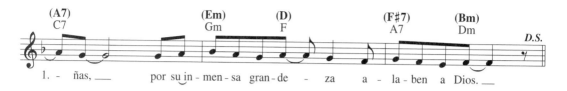

1. - ñas, ___ por su in - men - sa gran - de - za a - la - ben a Dios. ___

ESTROFA/VERSE 2

2. A - la - ben con trom - pe - tas y cuer - no. A - la - ben con cí - ta - ra y ar -

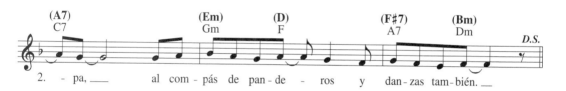

2. - pa, ___ al com - pás de pan - de - ros y dan - zas tam - bién. ___

ESTROFA/VERSE 3

3. A - la - ben con la - úd y con flau - ta. A - la - ben con pla - ti - llos so - no -

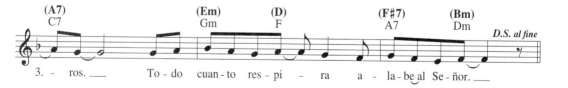

3. - ros. ___ To - do cuan - to res - pi - ra a - la - be al Se - ñor. ___

SUGGESTED COMMON PSALMS

This is a list of Common Responsorial Psalms suggested for each Sunday or Feast.

Sunday/Feast	Cycle / Psalm		
	A	B	C
Advent 1	122	130	25
Advent 2	72	85	85
Advent 3	25	27	145
Advent 4	85	91	85
Christmas	98	98	98
Holy Family	19	19	19
Mary, Mother of God	145	145	145
Epiphany	72	72	72
Baptism of the Lord	72	72	72
Ash Wednesday	51	51	51
Lent 1	51	25	91
Lent 2	145	95	27
Lent 3	95	19	103
Lent 4	72	130	34
Lent 5	130	51	27
Passion Sunday	22	22	22
Holy Thursday	34	34	34
Good Friday	22	22	22
Easter Vigil (1)	104	104	104
Easter Vigil (2)	25	25	25
Easter Vigil (3)	136	136	136
Easter Vigil (4)	103	103	103
Easter Vigil (5)	63	63	63
Easter Vigil (6)	19	19	19
Easter Vigil (7)	51	51	51
Easter Vigil (8)	118	118	118
Easter 1, 2, 3	118	118	118
Easter 4	63	118	100
Easter 5	100	145	145
Easter 6	66	98	27
Ascension	47	47	47
Easter 7	27	103	130
Pentecost	104	104	104
Trinity	145	103	145
Corpus Christi	34	34	34
Sacred Heart	103	63	100

Sundays of Ordinary Time			
	A	B	C
2nd	98	122	98
3rd	27	25	19
4th	85	95	85
5th	27	63	27
6th	19	130	85
7th	103	51	103
8th	63	103	19
9th	63	19	122
10th	51	130	130
11th	100	104	51
12th	25	136	63
13th	91	103	25
14th	145	95	66
15th	104	85	19
16th	130	100	34
17th	19	145	103
18th	145	104	95
19th	85	34	100
20th	27	34	25
21st	100	34	66
22nd	63	19	91
23rd	95	98	19
24th	103	91	51
25th	145	130	25
26th	25	19	85
27th	34	19	95
28th	34	27	98
29th	98	22	130
30th	103	91	34
31st	95	103	145
32nd	63	100	118
33rd	25	25	98
34th	100	72	122

Canticle of Zechariah

Based on Luke 1:68–79

Christopher Walker

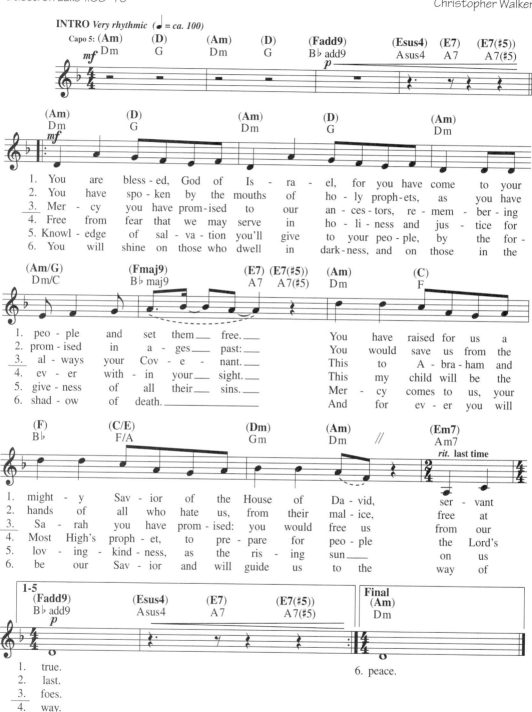

94 Canticle of Zachary

Based on Luke 1:68–79
Adapted by Carl P. Daw Jr.

Tom Tomaszek

VERSE 3

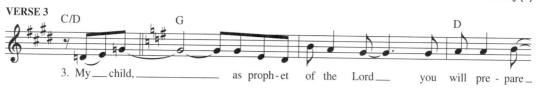

3. My ___ child, ___ as proph-et of the Lord ___ you will pre - pare ___

3. ___ the way, ___ to ___ tell ___ God's peo - ple they are saved ___ from

3. sin's e - ter - nal sway. ___ Then shall God's mer - cy from on high ___ shine

3. forth and nev - er cease ___ to drive a - way ___ the gloom of death ___

FINAL REFRAIN

3. ___ and lead us in - to ___ peace. ___ Blest ___ be ___ the God of

Is - ra - el, ___ the ev - er - liv - ing Lord! ___

95 Holy Is His Name

(Canticle of Mary)

Magnificat
Based on Luke 1:46–55

John Michael Talbot
Harmony by Rick Modlin

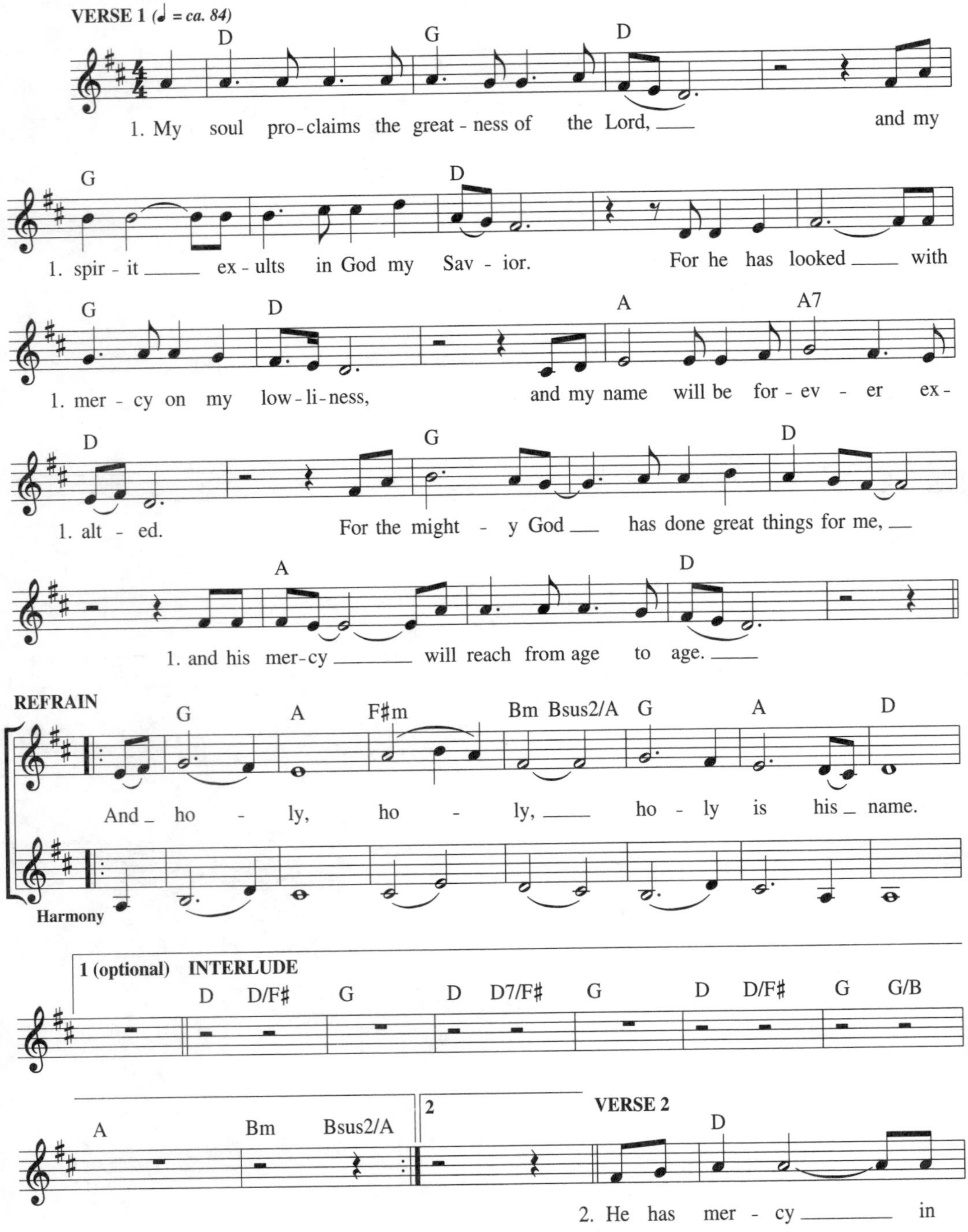

VERSE 1 (♩ = ca. 84)
D G D
1. My soul pro-claims the great - ness of the Lord, ___ and my
G D
1. spir - it ___ ex - ults in God my Sav - ior. For he has looked ___ with
G D A A7
1. mer - cy on my low - li - ness, and my name will be for - ev - er ex -
D G D
1. alt - ed. For the might - y God ___ has done great things for me, ___
A D
1. and his mer - cy ___ will reach from age to age. ___
REFRAIN
G A F#m Bm Bsus2/A G A D
And _ ho - ly, ho - ly, ___ ho - ly is his _ name.
Harmony
1 (optional) INTERLUDE
D D/F# G D D7/F# G D D/F# G G/B
A Bm Bsus2/A
2
VERSE 2
D
2. He has mer - cy ___ in

REFRAIN

FINAL REFRAIN

96

Holy Is Your Name
(Canticle of Mary)

Magnificat
Based on Luke 1:46–55

WILD MOUNTAIN THYME
Arranged by David Haas

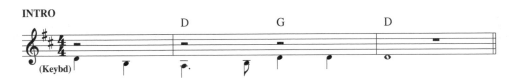

1. My ____ soul is filled with joy ____ as I
2. I am low - ly as a child, ____ but I
3. I pro - claim the pow'r of God, ____ you do
4. To the hun - gry you give food, ____ send the
5. In your love you now ful - fill ____ what you

1. sing to God my sav - ior: you have looked up - on your
2. know from this day for - ward that my name will be re -
3. mar - vels for your ser - vants; though you scat - ter the proud
4. rich a - way ____ emp - ty. In your mer - cy you are
5. prom - ised to your peo - ple. I will praise you, Lord, my

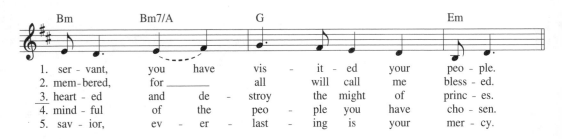

1. ser - vant, you have vis - it - ed your peo - ple.
2. mem - bered, for ____ all will call me bless - ed.
3. heart - ed and de - stroy the might of princ - es.
4. mind - ful of the peo - ple you have cho - sen.
5. sav - ior, ev - er - last - ing is your mer - cy.

REFRAIN

And ____ ho - ly is your name through ___ all gen - er -
a - tions! Ev - er - last - ing is your mer - cy to the
peo - ple you have cho - sen, and ____ ho - ly is your
name. (Keybd)

GATHERING & SENDING SONGS

97 Alleluia! Sing to Jesus

Based on HYFRYDOL
Rowland H. Prichard, 1811–1887
Arranged by Cyprian Consiglio

William Dix, 1837–1898, alt.

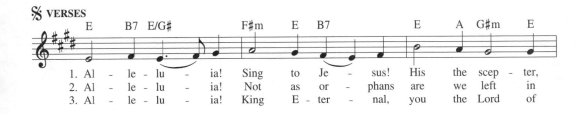

1. Al - le - lu - ia! Sing to Je - sus! His the scep - ter,
2. Al - le - lu - ia! Not as or - phans are we left in
3. Al - le - lu - ia! King E - ter - nal, you the Lord of

1. his ___ the throne. Al - le - lu - ia! His the tri - umph,
2. sor - row now; Al - le - lu - ia! He is near ___ us,
3. lords ___ we own. Al - le - lu - ia! Son of Ma - ry,

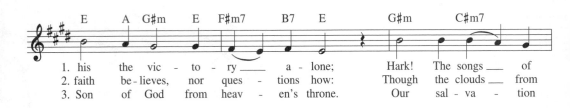

1. his the vic - to - ry ___ a - lone; Hark! The songs ___ of
2. faith be - lieves, nor ques - tions how: Though the clouds ___ from
3. Son of God from heav - en's throne. Our sal - va - tion

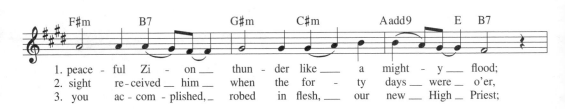

1. peace - ful Zi - on ___ thun - der like ___ a might - y ___ flood;
2. sight re - ceived ___ him ___ when the for - ty days ___ were ___ o'er,
3. you ac - com - plished, ___ robed in flesh, ___ our new ___ High ___ Priest;

1. Je - sus out __ of ev - 'ry na - tion   has re - deemed __ us __
2. shall __ our hearts __ for - get __ his prom - ise,   "I am with __ you __
3. here __ on earth __ both priest __ and vic - tim   in the Eu - cha -

1. by his __ blood.
2. ev - er - more"? _____
3. - ris - tic __ feast. _____

*Optional melody.

98 Age to Age

Verse 1 based on Isaiah 40:31
Verse 2 based on Matthew 6:28
Verse 3 based on Matthew 11:28–30

Janet Vogt

Gathering & Sending Songs

99 Alleluia! Alleluia! Let the Holy Anthem Rise

Anonymous; probably American, ca. 1887, alt.

Timothy R. Smith

Gathering & Sending Songs

100 At the Name of Jesus

Refrain text: Caroline Maria Noel, 1817–1877
Verses text adapted from Philippians 2 by Christopher Walker

Christopher Walker

At the name of Je - sus, __ ev - 'ry knee __ shall bow, ev - 'ry

tongue con - fess him: __ King of glo - ry now. __

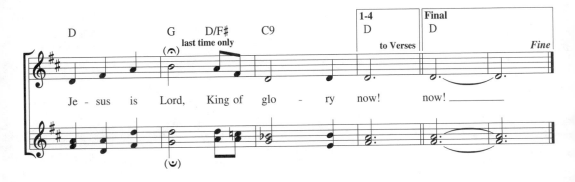

Je - sus is Lord, King of glo - ry now! now! __

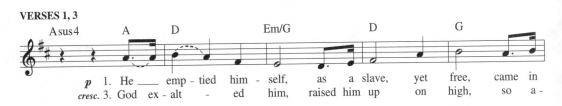

p 1. He __ emp - tied him - self, as a slave, yet free, came in
cresc. 3. God ex - alt - ed him, raised him up on high, so a -

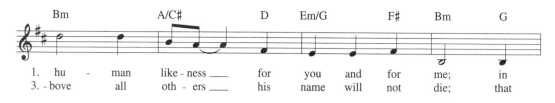

1. hu - man like - ness ___ for you and for me; in
3. - bove all oth - ers ___ his name will not die; that

1. hu - man like - ness ___ for you and for me. ___
3. name we hon - or ___ and glo - ri - fy. ___

VERSES 2, 4

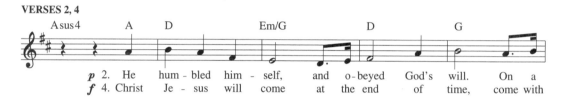

p 2. He hum - bled him - self, and o - beyed God's will. On a
f 4. Christ Je - sus will come at the end of time, come with

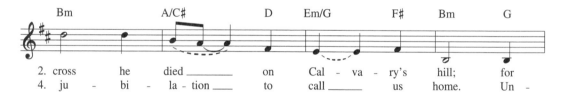

2. cross he died ___ on Cal - va - ry's hill; for
4. ju - bi - la - tion ___ to call ___ us home. Un -

2. you and me he o - beyed ___ God's will. ___
4. til that day you and I will pro - claim: ___

101 Beyond the Days

Ricky Manalo
Harmony by Craig Kingsbury

VERSES

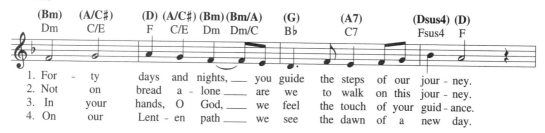

1. For - ty days and nights, ___ you guide the steps of our jour - ney.
2. Not on bread a - lone ___ are we to walk on this jour - ney.
3. In your hands, O God, ___ we feel the touch of your guid - ance.
4. On our Lent - en path ___ we see the dawn of a new day.

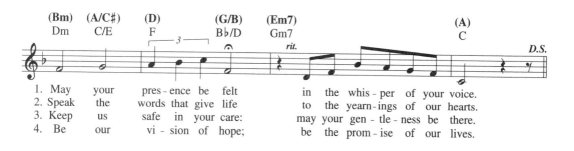

1. May your pres - ence be felt in the whis - per of your voice.
2. Speak the words that give life to the yearn-ings of our hearts.
3. Keep us safe in your care: may your gen - tle - ness be there.
4. Be our vi - sion of hope; be the prom - ise of our lives.

102 By the Waking of Our Hearts

Verses based on the Pentecost Sequence,
Veni Sancte Spiritus

Ricky Manalo

VERSES

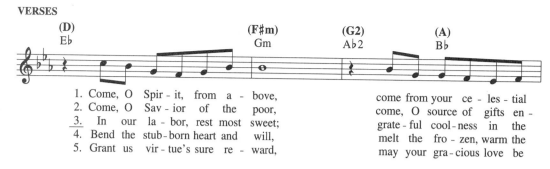

1. Come, O Spir - it, from a - bove,   come from your ce - les - tial
2. Come, O Sav - ior of the poor,   come, O source of gifts en -
3. In our la - bor, rest most sweet;   grate - ful cool - ness in the
4. Bend the stub - born heart and will,   melt the fro - zen, warm the
5. Grant us vir - tue's sure re - ward,   may your gra - cious love be

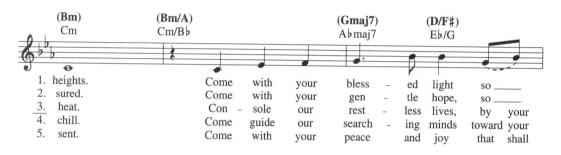

1. heights.   Come with your bless - ed light so _____
2. sured.   Come with your gen - tle hope, so _____
3. heat.   Con - sole our rest - less lives, by your
4. chill.   Come guide our search - ing minds toward your
5. sent.   Come with your peace and joy that shall

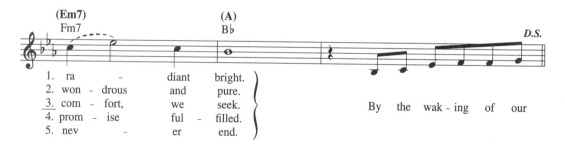

1. ra - diant bright.
2. won - drous and pure.
3. com - fort, we seek.
4. prom - ise ful - filled.
5. nev - er end.

By the wak - ing of our

103 Celebrate Youth

Steve Angrisano

INTRO (♩ = ca. 120)

1. We gath-er to-geth - er as chil-dren of __ our God. _____ We
1. take our place __ at the ta - ble of __ the Lord. __
1. We come with a sto - ry; young __ and old, ___ we lift __ our voice __
1. _____ to cel - e - brate __ the gift ___ of youth __ pro - claimed. __

REFRAIN

Cel - e - brate life! Cel - e - brate love! All of the dreams __
__ of our to - mor - rows. Cel - e - brate joy! For all of the gifts __

Amazing Grace

Verses 1–4, John Newton, 1725–1807
Verse 5, anon., from *A Collection of Sacred Ballads*, 1790

NEW BRITAIN, CM
Columbian Harmony, 1829

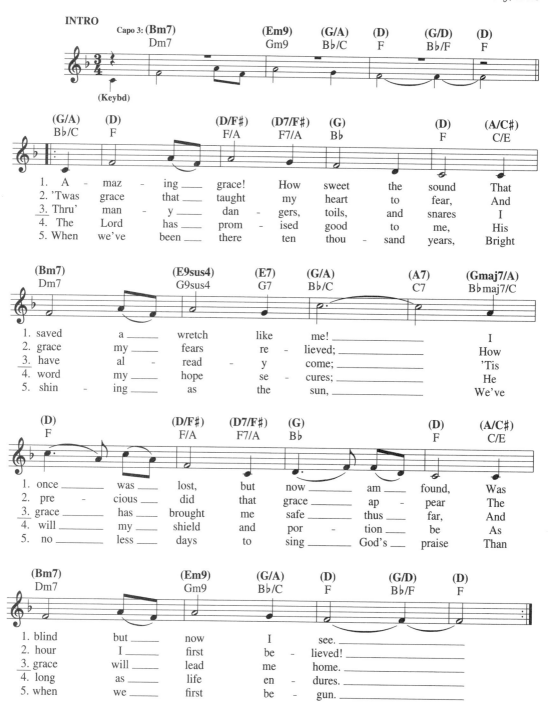

1. A - maz - ing ____ grace! How sweet the sound That
2. 'Twas grace that ____ taught my heart to fear, And
3. Thru' man - y ____ dan - gers, toils, and snares I
4. The Lord has ____ prom - ised good to me, His
5. When we've been ____ there ten thou - sand years, Bright

1. saved a ____ wretch like me! ____ I
2. grace my ____ fears re - lieved; ____ How
3. have al - read - y come; ____ 'Tis
4. word my ____ hope se - cures; ____ He
5. shin - ing ____ as the sun, ____ We've

1. once ____ was lost, but now ____ am ____ found, Was
2. pre - cious ____ did that grace ____ ap - pear The
3. grace has ____ brought me safe ____ thus ____ far, And
4. will ____ my ____ shield and por - tion ____ be As
5. no ____ less days to sing ____ God's ____ praise Than

1. blind but ____ now I see.
2. hour I ____ first be - lieved!
3. grace will ____ lead me home.
4. long as ____ life en - dures.
5. when we ____ first be - gun.

Gathering & Sending Songs

105 Christ, Be Our Light

Bernadette Farrell

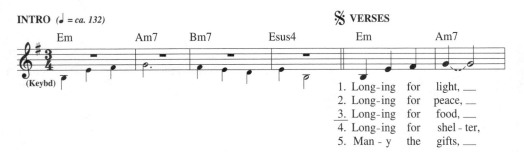

INTRO (♩ = ca. 132)   𝄋 VERSES

Em   Am7   Bm7   Esus4   Em   Am7

(Keybd)

1. Long-ing for light, ___
2. Long-ing for peace, ___
3. Long-ing for food, ___
4. Long-ing for shel - ter,
5. Man - y the gifts, ___

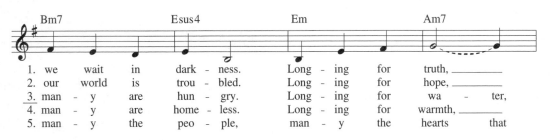

Bm7   Esus4   Em   Am7

1. we wait in dark - ness. Long - ing for truth, ___
2. our world is trou - bled. Long - ing for hope, ___
3. man - y are hun - gry. Long - ing for wa - ter,
4. man - y are home - less. Long - ing for warmth, ___
5. man - y the peo - ple, man - y the hearts that

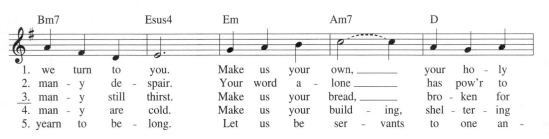

Bm7   Esus4   Em   Am7   D

1. we turn to you. Make us your own, ___ your ho - ly
2. man - y de - spair. Your word a - lone ___ has pow'r to
3. man - y still thirst. Make us your bread, ___ bro - ken for
4. man - y are cold. Make us your build - ing, shel - ter - ing
5. yearn to be - long. Let us be ser - vants to one an -

G   C   Am   Dsus4   D

1. peo - ple, light for the world to see. ___
2. save us. Make us your liv - ing voice. ___
3. oth - ers, shared un - til all are fed. ___
4. oth - ers, walls made of liv - ing stone. ___
5. oth - er, mak - ing your king - dom come. ___

REFRAIN

Melody: Christ, be our light! Shine in our hearts. Shine through the

Harmony: Christ, be our light! Shine out through the

Melody: dark - ness. Christ, be our light! Shine in your

Harmony: dark, shine! Christ, be our light! Shine in your

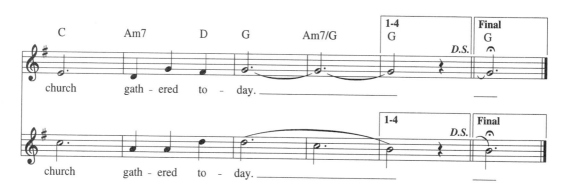

Melody: church gath - ered to - day.

Harmony: church gath - ered to - day.

106 City of God

Based on Isaiah 9, 40; 1 John 1

Dan Schutte

Lead Me, Lord

Matthew 5:3–12; 7:7, 13
John 14:6

John D. Becker

Gathering & Sending Songs

108 Deo Gratias

Based on Psalm 145:2, 4, 9, 10

Peter Rubalcava

4. *Que se pro-cla-me tu glo-ria y lo ma-ra-vi-llo-so que e-res.* ___

5. Let all your works give you thanks, and ___ let all your faith-ful ones bless you. ___

6. *Que te a-la-ben tus o-bras, que te ben-di-gan to-dos ___ tus fie-les.* ___

7. God is good to all, com-pas-sion-ate toward all his works. ___

8. *Dios es bue-no con to-dos, y Dios a-ma a to-das sus cria-tu-ras.* ___

Find Us Ready

Tom Booth

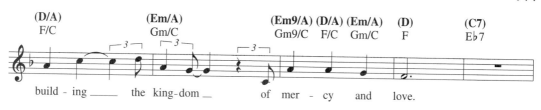

build - ing _____ the king-dom _ of mer - cy and love.

	1-3	Final		Optional Final Ending		
(Bb7)	**(A7)**	**(A)**	**(D)**	**(A7)**	**(D)**	to Optional
Db7	C7 to Verses	C7	F Fine	C7	F	Coda to Optional

VERSES

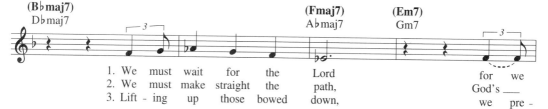

1. We must wait for the Lord   for we
2. We must make straight the path,   God's ___
3. Lift - ing up those bowed down,   we pre -

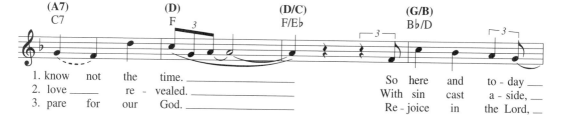

1. know not the time. _____ So here and to - day ___
2. love ___ re - vealed. _____ With sin cast a - side, ___
3. pare for our God. _____ Re - joice in the Lord, ___

1. __   we gath - er and pray, ___   dis - cov - er - ing
2. __   God's mer - cy a - live, ___   fear not for
3. __   for hope has been born ___   in hearts where our

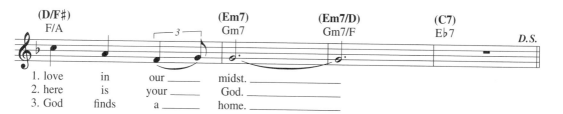

1. love in our _____ midst. _____
2. here is your _____ God. _____
3. God finds a _____ home.

OPTIONAL CODA ($\,d\,$ = ca. 128)

Go Ye Out

110

Tom Booth

*Capo 1 begins after Verse 2.

Gathering & Sending Songs

*KiSwahili: Go and tell the whole world!

*French: Go, tell all the nations!

Gathering & Sending Songs

111   Gather Your People

Bob Hurd
Harmony by Craig Kingsbury

Based on 1 Corinthians 12; Isaiah 2:3–4; 11:9

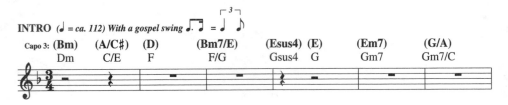

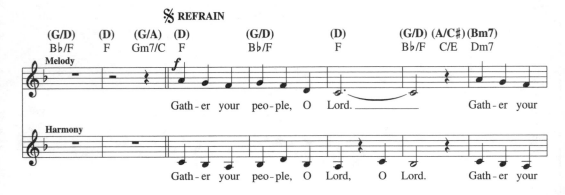

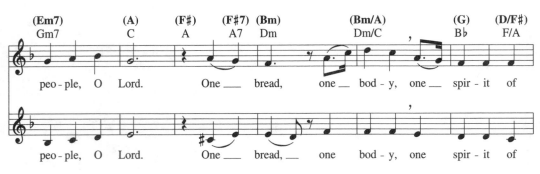

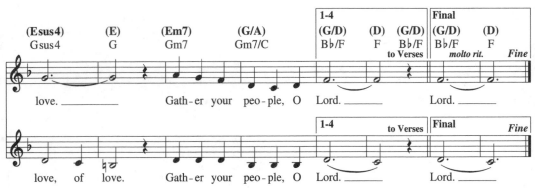

VERSES

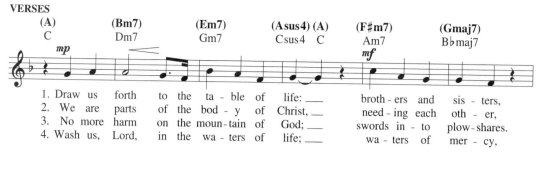

1. Draw us forth to the ta - ble of life: ___ broth - ers and sis - ters,
2. We are parts of the bod - y of Christ, ___ need - ing each oth - er,
3. No more harm on the moun - tain of God; ___ swords in - to plow - shares.
4. Wash us, Lord, in the wa - ters of life; ___ wa - ters of mer - cy,

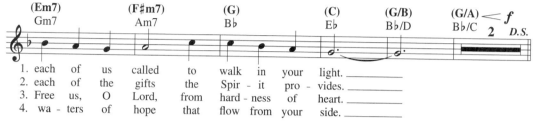

1. each of us called to walk in your light. _____
2. each of the gifts the Spir - it pro - vides. _____
3. Free us, O Lord, from hard - ness of heart. _____
4. wa - ters of hope that flow from your side. _____

112 Go Light Your World

Chris Rice

VERSES 1, 2

1. There is a candle in ev'ry soul; some brightly burning,
2. Frus-trat-ed broth-er, see how he's tried to light his own can-dle

1. some dark and cold. There is a Spir-it who brings a
2. some oth-er way. See now your sis-ter, she's been robbed and

1. fire, ig-nites a can-dle and makes his home.
2. lied to, still holds a can-dle with-out a flame.

REFRAIN

So, car-ry your can-dle, run to the dark-ness, seek out the

1. hope-less, con-fused and torn.
2. lone-ly, the tired and worn.

Hold out your can-dle for all to

see it. Take your can-dle and go light your world. Take your

1. can-dle and go light your world.
2. can-dle and go light your

113 Go Make a Difference

Based on Matthew 5:13–16

Steve Angrisano and Tom Tomaszek

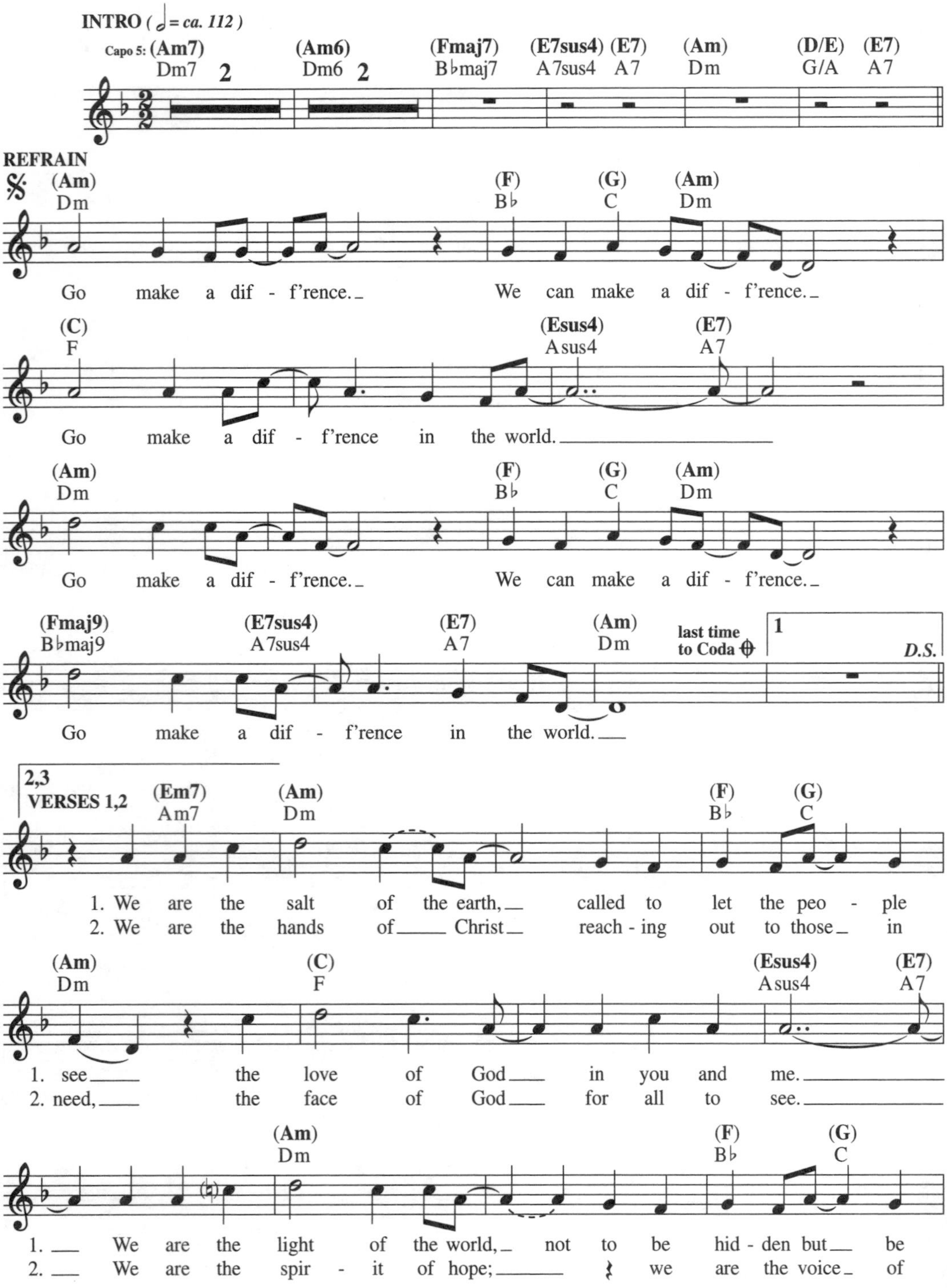

INTRO (𝅗𝅥 = ca. 112)
Capo 5: (Am7) Dm7 2 (Am6) Dm6 2 (Fmaj7) B♭maj7 (E7sus4) A7sus4 (E7) A7 (Am) Dm (D/E) G/A (E7) A7
REFRAIN
(Am) Dm (F) B♭ (G) C (Am) Dm
Go make a dif - f'rence. We can make a dif - f'rence.
(C) F (Esus4) Asus4 (E7) A7
Go make a dif - f'rence in the world.
(Am) Dm (F) B♭ (G) C (Am) Dm
Go make a dif - f'rence. We can make a dif - f'rence.
(Fmaj9) B♭maj9 (E7sus4) A7sus4 (E7) A7 (Am) Dm
Go make a dif - f'rence in the world.
last time to Coda
1
D.S.
2,3
VERSES 1,2
(Em7) Am7 (Am) Dm (F) B♭ (G) C
1. We are the salt of the earth, called to let the peo - ple
2. We are the hands of Christ reach - ing out to those in
(Am) Dm (C) F (Esus4) Asus4 (E7) A7
1. see the love of God in you and me.
2. need, the face of God for all to see.
(Am) Dm (F) B♭ (G) C
1. We are the light of the world, not to be hid - den but be
2. We are the spir - it of hope; we are the voice of

114   Go, Tell It on the Mountain

American Negro Songs and Spirituals, 1940
John W. Work, Jr., 1871–1925, alt.

Spiritual
Arranged by Peter Quint

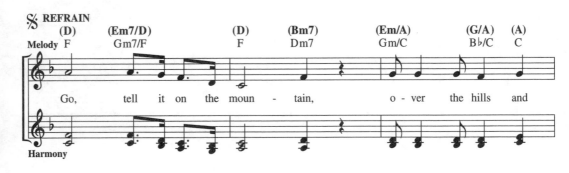

Final

(D/A) (Em/A) (A7) (D)
F/C Gm/C C7 F

Fine

Je - sus Christ____ is born.

VERSES

(D) (Em7) (F#m7) (Bm7) (Em7) (G/A) (D) (G/A)
F Gm7 Am7 Dm7 Gm7 B♭/C F B♭/C

1. While shep-herds kept their watch-ing____ o'er si - lent flocks by night, be -
2. The shep-herds feared and trem-bled____ when high a - bove the earth rang
3. And lo, when they had heard it,____ they all bowed down and prayed; they
4. Down in a low - ly man - ger____ the hum - ble Christ was born, and

(D) (Em7) (F#m7) (Bm7) (Esus4) (E) (G/A) (A7)
F Gm7 Am7 Dm7 Gsus4 G B♭/C C7

D.S.

1. hold, through - out the heav - ens____ there shone a ho - ly light.____
2. out the an - gel cho - rus____ that hailed our Sav - ior's birth.____
3. trav - eled on to - geth - er____ to where the babe was laid.____
4. God sent us sal - va - tion____ that bless - ed Christ - mas morn.____

115   God, Creator, God Most High

Janet Vogt

VERSES: Cantor

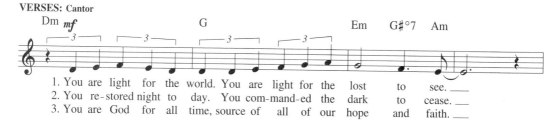

1. You are light for the world. You are light for the lost to see. ____
2. You re-stored night to day. You com-mand-ed the dark to cease. ____
3. You are God for all time, source of all of our hope and faith. ____

1. Out of dark-ness we come to the light of your love, for your word is a
2. By your prom-ise of love we shall not walk in fear. We shall walk in the
3. Call your peo-ple a-gain to go forth and re-new all the earth with the

1. lamp _____ un - to _____ our feet _____ to guide __ us.
2. light _____ of hope _____ and peace _____ to guide __ us.
3. strength _____ of love _____ and grace _____ to guide __ us.

116 Holy Spirit

Verses 1 & 2 based on Isaiah 11:2
Verses 3–6 based on the Pentecost Sequence

Ken Canedo

1. un - der - stand - ing heart._____ Give us a spir - it of knowl-
2. judg - ment that___ is wise._____ Give us a spir - it of rev -
3. hope to all___ the poor._____ Spir - it of jus - tice and mer -
4. lift our hearts___ this day._____ Spir - it of all___ un - der - stand -
5. lift us from___ our sor - row.___ Spir - it of peace___ and for - give -
6. stub - born heart___ and will._____ Spir - it of trust___ and of car -

come in - to___ our lives._____ Ho - ly___

1. - edge,_____ and lead us to___ the truth._____
2. - 'rence,_____ of won - der and___ of awe._____
3. - cy,_____ come o - pen ev - 'ry door._____
4. - ing,_____ O help us know___ your way._____
5. - ness,_____ O help us face___ to - mor - row.___
6. - ing,_____ O melt us, warm___ our chill._____

Spir - it, ___ make us tru - ly wise._____

D.S.

237

Gathering & Sending Songs

117 How Can I Keep from Singing

Anonymous, from *Bright Jewels for the Sunday School*, 1869
Adapted by Robert Lowry (1826–1899)

ENDLESS SONG
Attributed to Robert Lowry

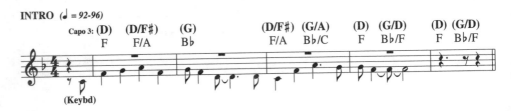

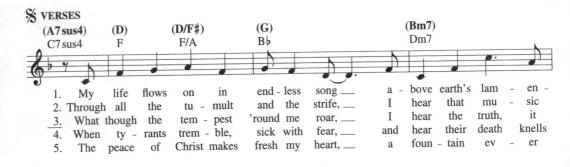

1. My life flows on in end - less song __ a - bove earth's lam - en -
2. Through all the tu - mult and the strife, __ I hear that mu - sic
3. What though the tem - pest 'round me roar, __ I hear the truth, it
4. When ty - rants trem - ble, sick with fear, __ and hear their death knells
5. The peace of Christ makes fresh my heart, __ a foun - tain ev - er

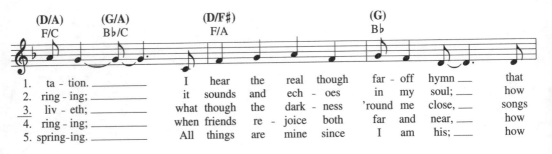

1. ta - tion. _____ I hear the real though far - off hymn __ that
2. ring - ing; _____ it sounds and ech - oes in my soul; __ how
3. liv - eth; _____ what though the dark - ness 'round me close, __ songs
4. ring - ing; _____ when friends re - joice both far and near, __ how
5. spring - ing. _____ All things are mine since I am his; __ how

REFRAIN

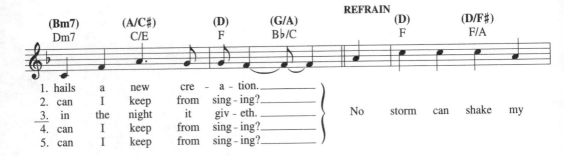

1. hails a new cre - a - tion. _____
2. can I keep from sing - ing? _____
3. in the night it giv - eth. _____ } No storm can shake my
4. can I keep from sing - ing? _____
5. can I keep from sing - ing? _____

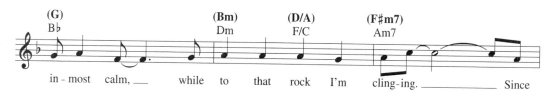

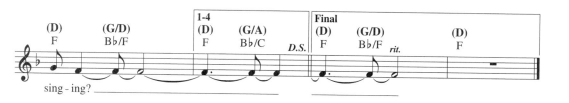

118   I Am the Light of the World

Based on John 8:12; Ephesians 5:14;
1 John 2:10; Matthew 5:14

Greg Hayakawa
Arranged by Craig Kingsbury

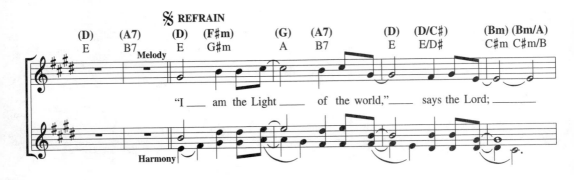

"I ___ am the Light ___ of the world," ___ says the Lord; ___

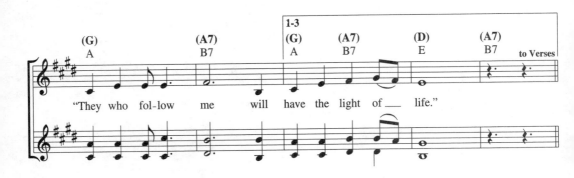

"They who fol-low me will have the light of ___ life."

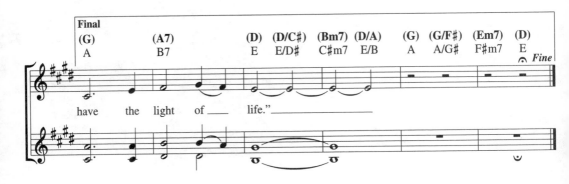

have the light of ___ life." ___

119 I Will Choose Christ

Tom Booth

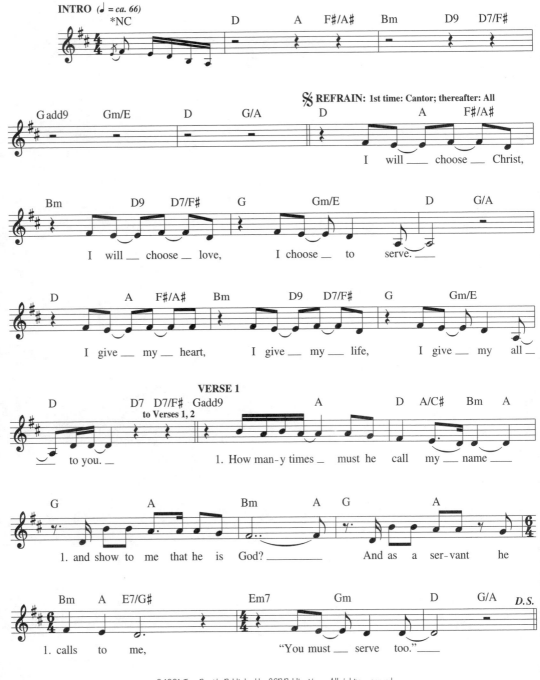

*Capo 1 begins at final refrain.

VERSE 2

2. Christ, my teach - er and heal - er,   teach my

2. heart and heal my soul.   And as I walk this

2. road with you,   teach me ___ to love. ___

REFRAIN

I will ___ choose ___ Christ,   I will ___ choose ___ love,   I choose ___

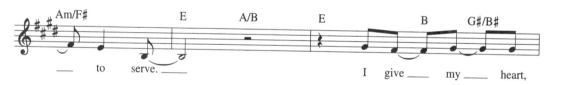

___ to serve. ___   I give ___ my ___ heart,

I give ___ my ___ life,   I give ___ my all ___ to you. _

VERSE 3

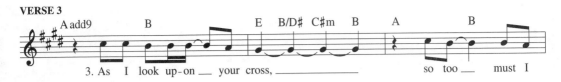

A add9   B   E   B/D♯   C♯m   B   A   B

3. As I look up-on ___ your cross, _____ so too ___ must I

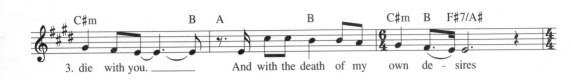

C♯m   B   A   B   C♯m   B   F♯7/A♯

3. die with you. _____ And with the death of my own de - sires

FINAL REFRAIN

Capo 1: **(E)**   **(B)**   **(G♯/B♯)**

F♯m7   Am   E   NC   F   C   A/C♯

3. I'll rise ___ with you. ___ I will ___ choose ___ Christ,

(C♯m)   **(E9)**   **(E7/G♯)**   **(A)**   **(Am/F♯)**   **(E)**   **(A/B)**   **(E)**

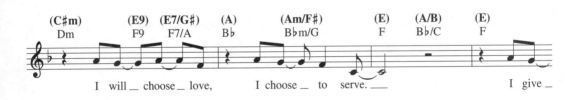

Dm   F9   F7/A   B♭   B♭m/G   F   B♭/C   F

I will ___ choose ___ love, I choose ___ to serve. ___ I give ___

(B)   **(G♯/B♯)**   **(C♯m)**   **(E9)**   **(E7/G♯)**   **(A)**   **(Am/F♯)**   **1** **(E)**

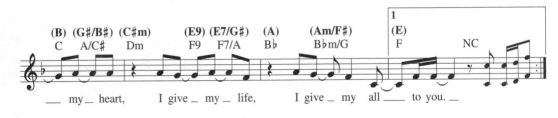

C   A/C♯   Dm   F9   F7/A   B♭   B♭m/G   F   NC

___ my ___ heart, I give ___ my ___ life, I give ___ my all ____ to you. ___

Final

(E)   **(E7/G♯)**   **(E7)**   **(A)**   **(Am/F♯)**   **(E)**

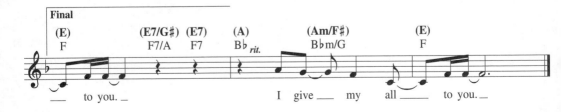

F   F7/A   F7   B♭ *rit.*   B♭m/G   F

___ to you. ___ I give ___ my all ____ to you. ___

Morning Has Broken

120

BUNESSAN
Traditional Gaelic Melody
Arranged by Rick Modlin

Eleanor Farjeon, 1881–1965

1. Morn - ing has bro - ken like the first morn - ing,
2. Sweet the rain's new fall, sun - lit from heav - en,
3. Mine is the sun - light! Mine is the morn - ing

1. Black - bird has spo - ken like the first bird.
2. Like the first dew - fall on the first grass.
3. Born of the one light E - den saw play!

1. Praise for the sing - ing! Praise for the morn - ing!
2. Praise for the sweet - ness of the wet gar - den,
3. Praise with e - la - tion, praise ev - 'ry morn - ing,

1. Praise for them, spring - ing fresh from the Word!
2. Sprung in com - plete - ness where his feet pass.
3. God's re - cre - a - tion of the new day!

Gathering & Sending Songs

121 In the Day of the Lord

Based on Isaiah 2, 25, 41

M.D. Ridge

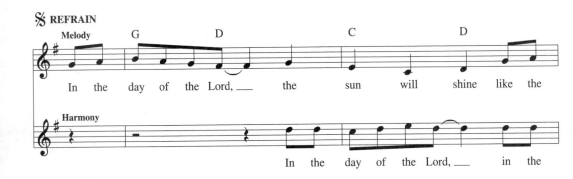

VERSES

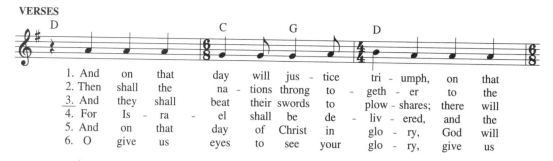

1. And on that day will jus - tice tri - umph, on that
2. Then shall the na - tions throng to - geth - er to the
3. And they shall beat their swords to plow - shares; there will
4. For Is - ra - el shall be de - liv - ered, and the
5. And on that day of Christ in glo - ry, God will
6. O give us eyes to see your glo - ry, give us

1. day will all be free: free from want, free from
2. moun - tain of the Lord: they shall walk in the
3. be an end to war: one in peace, one in
4. des - ert lands will bloom. Say to all, "Do not
5. wipe a - way our tears, and the dead shall rise
6. hearts to un - der - stand. Let our ears hear your

1. fear, _____ free to live! _____
2. light _____ of the Lord! _____
3. love, _____ one in God! _____
4. fear. Here is your God!" _____
5. up _____ from their graves! _____
6. voice _____ 'til you come! _____

122 In This Place

Victoria Thomson

Trevor Thomson

123 Jesus Christ Is Risen Today

Verses 1, 2: Latin carol, 14th cent.
Verse 3: Anonymous

Cyprian Consiglio

251   *Gathering & Sending Songs*

124 Lead Us to the Water: Dismissal

Tom Kendzia and Gary Daigle

125

Let the River Flow

Darrel Evans

Let the poor man — say, — "I am rich in him." — Let the lost man — say, — "I am found in him." — Oh, let the riv - er flow. _____ Let the blind man — say, — "I can see a-gain." — Let the dead man — say, — "I am born a-gain." — Oh, let the riv - er flow. _____ Oh, let the riv - er flow. —

REFRAIN

Gathering & Sending Songs

126
Lift Up Your Hearts/ Behold the Glory of God

Roc O'Connor, SJ
Harmony by Bob Dufford, SJ
Adapted by Chris Deily and Roc O'Connor, SJ

Lift up your hearts to the Lord, — / Be - hold the glo - ry of God, —
Lift up your hearts, — / Be - hold your God, —

praise God's gra - cious mer — cy! / Sing out your joy to the Lord, — whose
the Day-Star a - ris - ing! / Christ Je - sus shines on the earth — with
praise God's all - gra - cious mer - cy, sing! / Sing out to God, — whose
O praise the Light a - ris-ing. See! / Christ shines on earth — with

love is en - dur - ing. / - ing.
mer - cy en - dur - ing! / - ing!

VERSES *"Lift Up Your Hearts"*

1. Shout with joy__ to the Lord, all the earth! Praise the name_ a-bove all
2. Let the earth__ wor-ship, sing - ing your praise. Praise the glo - ry of your
3. God's right hand__ made a path through the night, split the wa - ters of the
4. Lis - ten now,__ all you ser - vants of God, as I tell__ of these great

*D tuning suggested.

1. names!   Say to God, "How won-drous your works,   how glo-rious your name!"
2. name!   Come and see what God has re - vealed;   bless God's ho - ly name!
3. sea.   All cre - a - tion, lift up your voice: "Our God set us free!"
4. works.   Bless-ed be the Lord of my life,   whose love shall en - dure!

VERSES *"Behold the Glory of God"*

1. Night of hope, __ night of glo - ry di - vine—   Dark - ness con -
2. Dance for joy __ all you an - gels of God,   Let the pow'rs __
3. Let the earth __ in its beau - ty re - joice,   Ra - diant as __
4. Robed a - bout __ in the light of the day,   Let the Church __
5. Bless - ed was __ the first fall from your grace,   Bless - ed was __
6. O how won - drous the gift of your love,   Ten - der gift __
7. O my God, __ you are wor - thy in - deed   To re - ceive __
8. God de - liv - ered our life from the snare   With a strong __
9. Through the fire __ and the wa - ter you led   With the dark -
10. Lift your hands, __ of - f'ring thanks un - to God,   Raise a hymn __
11. With a shout, __ wa - ter fled from the sea,   Paths were o -
12. O re - mem - ber your prom - ise, O God;   Let your mer -

1. - quered ev - er - more.   Christ tri - um - phant
2. __ of heav'n ex - ult.   All cre - a - tion,
3. __ the morn - ing sky.   Chains of death __ lie
4. __ take up its praise.   Sa - cred walls __ re -
5. __ the fate - ful sin.   Bless - ed more __ the
6. __ on our be - half: To re - deem __ a
7. __ our grate - ful song.   We ac - claim __ the
8. __ and might - y hand;   Set us free __ from
9. - ness round a - bout.   Death was near; __ the
10. __ of end - less praise: Bless - ed be __ the
11. - pened by your Word.   Far be - yond __ our
12. - cy still re - main: Save your peo - ple who

1. shines on the earth   With joy that en - dures.
2. join now in song: "Sal - va - tion is won!"
3. shat - tered this night—   Christ's vic - t'ry com - plete!
4. sound with the voice   Of God's ho - ly ones.
5. *blood of the Cross: Our God set us free.
6. slave low - ly born   You gave us the Christ.
7. deeds of your hand: "Praise God ev - er - more!"
8. all of our foes   To wor - ship The Name.
9. snare was re - leased;   Our God set us free!
10. Lord of our lives,   Whose mer - cy en - dures.
11. thoughts or de - sires,   Your mer - cy is sure!
12. cry out to you,   "O God, set us free!"

*Verse 5 alternate text: vic-t'ry of Christ

127

Lord of All Hopefulness

Jan Struther (1901–1953)

Timothy R. Smith

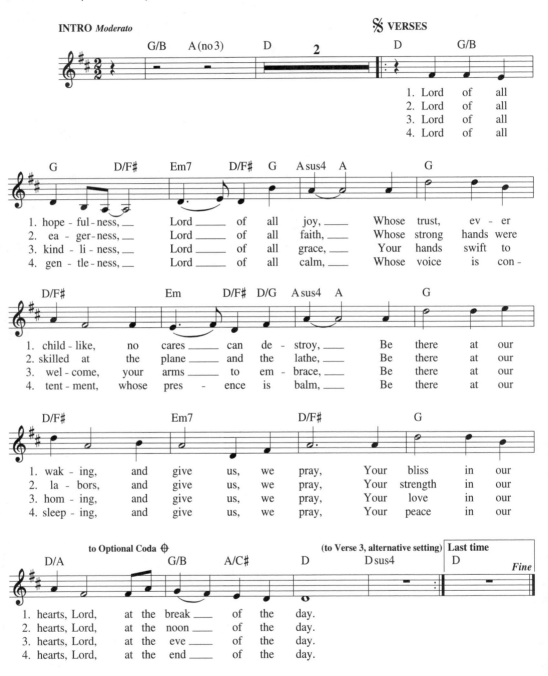

VERSE 3 (Alternative Setting)

3. Lord of all kind-li-ness, — Lord ___ of all grace, Your

3. hands swift to wel-come, your arms ___ to em-brace, ___ Be

3. there at our hom-ing, and give ___ us, we pray, Your

3. love in our hearts, Lord, at the eve ___ of the day. ___

D.S. al Coda

CODA (Optional)

4. end ___ of the day. ___

Ah ___

Ah ___

Ah ___   Ah ___

Gathering & Sending Songs

128 Lord of the Dance

Sydney Carter

SHAKER SONG
Adapted by Sydney Carter

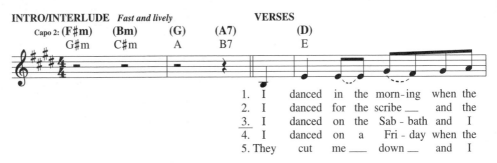

1. I danced in the morn-ing when the
2. I danced for the scribe ___ and the
3. I danced on the Sab-bath and I
4. I danced on a Fri-day when the
5. They cut me ___ down ___ and I

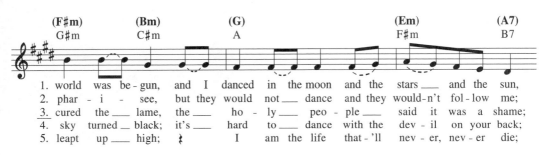

1. world was be-gun, and I danced in the moon and the stars ___ and the sun,
2. phar-i-see, but they would not ___ dance and they would-n't fol-low me;
3. cured the ___ lame, the ___ ho-ly ___ peo-ple ___ said it was a shame;
4. sky turned ___ black; it's ___ hard to ___ dance with the dev-il on your back;
5. leapt up ___ high; I am the life that-'ll nev-er, nev-er die;

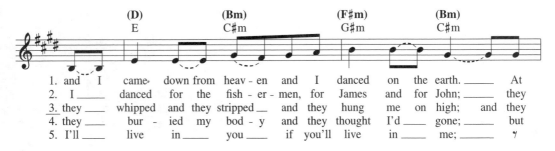

1. and I came down from heav-en and I danced on the earth. ___ At
2. I ___ danced for the fish-er-men, for James and for John; ___ they
3. they ___ whipped and they stripped ___ and they hung me on high; and they
4. they ___ bur-ied my bod-y and they thought I'd ___ gone; ___ but
5. I'll ___ live in ___ you ___ if you'll live in ___ me; ___

1. Beth-le-hem I ___ had my birth.
2. came with ___ me and the dance went on.
3. left me ___ there on a cross to die.   "Dance, then, wher-ev-er you may be;
4. I am the Dance and I still go on.
5. "I am the Lord of the Dance," said he.

I am the Lord of the Dance," said he. "And I'll lead you all, wher-ev-er you may be, And I'll

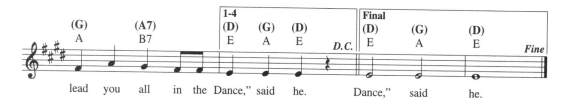

lead you all in the Dance," said he.   Dance," said he.

129 Malo! Malo! Thanks Be to God

Misa del Mundo
Jesse Manibusan

INTRO (♩ = ca. 140)

REFRAIN

*Malo! Malo! Thanks be to God! *Malo! Malo! Thanks be to God!

O-bri-ga-do! Al-le-lu-ia! O-bri-ga-do! Al-le-lu-ia!

¡Gra-ci-as! Kam sa ham ni da! ¡Gra-ci-as! Kam sa ham ni da!

(to Verses)
Ma-lo! Ma-lo! Thanks be to God! Ma-lo! Ma-lo! Thanks be to God!
1. Si

Last time (repeat *ad lib.*)
Ma-lo! Ma-lo! Thanks be to God! Ma-lo! Ma-lo! Thanks be to God!

VERSE 1

Cantor 1. Yu-'us ma-a'-se!

All 1. Si Yu-'us ma-a'-se!

*See pronunciation guide on p. 68.

Gathering & Sending Songs

130 Nadie en el Sepulcro/No One in the Tomb

Jaime Cortez

*Guitar tacet last two times.

GOSPEL VERSE 1a: 1st time: Cantor; Choir repeats

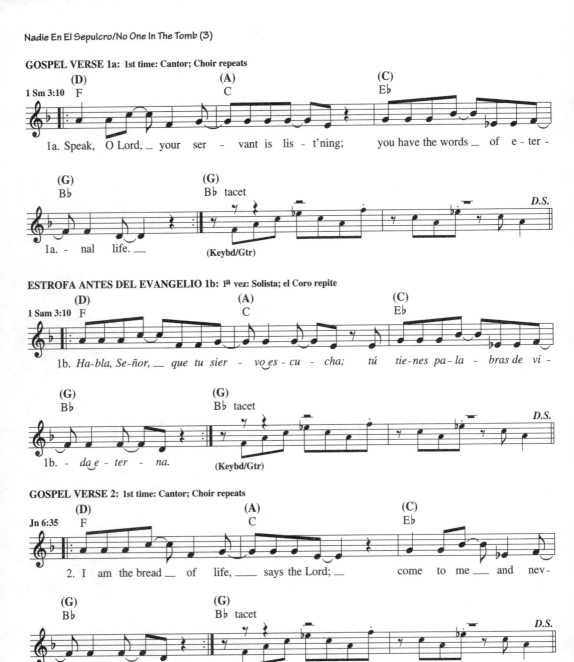

1a. Speak, O Lord, __ your ser - vant is lis - t'ning; you have the words __ of e - ter -

1a. - nal life. __ (Keybd/Gtr)

ESTROFA ANTES DEL EVANGELIO 1b: 1ª vez: Solista; el Coro repite

1b. Ha-bla, Se-ñor, __ que tu sier - vo es - cu - cha; tú tie-nes pa - la - bras de vi -

1b. - da e - ter - na. (Keybd/Gtr)

GOSPEL VERSE 2: 1st time: Cantor; Choir repeats

2. I am the bread __ of life, __ says the Lord; __ come to me __ and nev-

2. - er hun - ger. (Keybd/Gtr)

Song of the Body of Christ

131

NO KE ANO' AHI' AHI
Traditional Hawaiian Song
Adapted by David Haas

David Haas

REFRAIN *Gently* (♩ = 80-84)

We _ come to share our sto-ry, we _ come to break the bread,
we _ come to know our ris-ing from the _ dead. _

VERSES

mp 1. We _ come _ as your peo-ple, we _ come _ as your own,
mp 2. We are called to heal the bro-ken, to be hope _ for the poor;
mp 3. Bread of life and cup of prom-ise, in this meal we all are one.
mf 4. You will lead and we shall fol-low, you will be the breath of life;
mf 5. We will live and sing your prais-es, "Al-le-lu-ia" is our song.

1. u-nit-ed with each oth-er, love _ finds a home. _
2. we are called to feed the hun-gry at _ our _ door. _
3. In our dy-ing and our ris-ing, may your king-dom come. _
4. liv-ing wa-ter, we are thirst-ing for _ your _ light. _
5. May we live in love and peace our whole _ life _ long. _

Play Refrain twice as an Intro.

Gathering & Sending Songs

132 One Spirit, One Church

Refrain: Maryanne Quinlivan, OSU
Verses: attributed to Rabanus Maurus, 776–856
Translation by Edward Caswall, 1814–1878, alt.

Kevin Keil

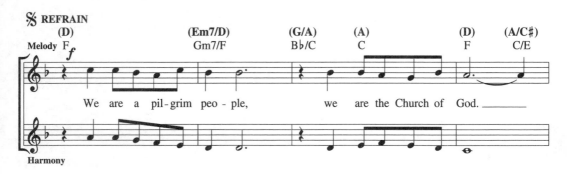

We are a pil-grim peo-ple, we are the Church of God. _____

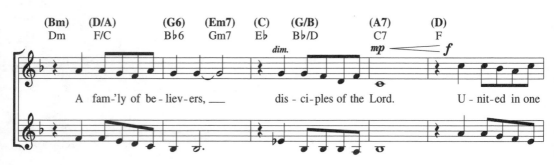

A fam'-ly of be-liev-ers, _____ dis-ci-ples of the Lord. U-nit-ed in one

spir-it, ig-nit-ed by the fire. _____ Still burn-ing through the a-ges,

VERSES *Tenderly*

(Dadd9) Fadd9 — (Em9/D) Gm9/F — (A) C — (D) F — (A/C♯) C/E (Bm9) Dm9 — (Em7) Gm7 — (D) F

mp

1. Come, Ho - ly Ghost, Cre - a - tor blest, _____ and in our hearts ____ take
2. O Com-fort - er, to thee we cry, _____ thou gift of God ____ sent

(C) E♭ — (A) C — (Dadd9) Fadd9 — (Em9/D) Gm9/F — (A) C

mf

1. up _____ thy rest; come with thy grace and heav'n - ly
2. from _____ on high. Thou font of life and fire of

(D) F — (F♯m) Am — (G) B♭ — (Em9) Gm9 (A7) C7 (D) F (G/D) B♭/F

f

D.S.

1. aid to fill the hearts which ___ thou hast made. _____
2. love, the soul's a - noint - ing ___ from a - bove. _____

133 Power of Peace

Jesse Manibusan

INTRO *With a driving beat* (♩ = ca. 104)

E G Dadd9 Aadd9 | **1** E G Dadd9 ‖ **2** E G Dadd9

𝄋 REFRAIN

E / G / Dadd9

We've got the pow - er of peace ___ in ev - 'ry word ___

Aadd9 / **1** E / G

___ and ev - 'ry deed. We've got the pow - er of peace.

Dadd9 / **2** E / G Dadd9 **to Coda** ⊕

___ We've got the pow - er of peace. ___

VERSES

Em / Dadd11 / Cadd9

1. The Church, ___ the Tem - ple, in ___ the Mosque ___ and ev - 'ry - where ___
2. Dis - crim - i - na - tion, prej - u - dice ___ is on ___ the rise. ___
3. In - doc - tri - na - ted to ___ the ec - o - nom - ic creed, ___

Dadd9 / Em / Dadd11

1. ___ two or three ___ are gath - ered, ___
2. ___ Her - i - tage ___ of ha - tred, ___
3. ___ peace is just ___ a pris - 'ner, ___

C6 / Bsus4 / **2/4** / **D.S.** / **4/4**

1. pow'r of peace ___ is grow - ing there. ___
2. will we ev - er re - al - ize? ___
3. waits for us ___ to set ___ her free. ___

⊕ **CODA**

E G Dadd9 Aadd9 | **1** E G Dadd9 ‖ **Final** E G Dadd9

Rain Down

Based on Psalm 33

Jaime Cortez

Play first eight measures as an Intro.

Gathering & Sending Songs

River of Glory

Dan Schutte

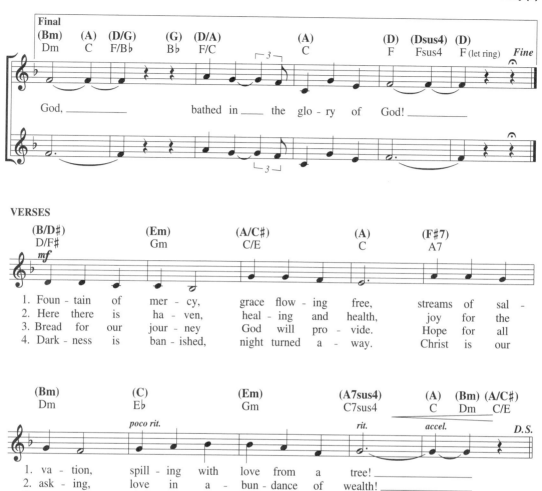

Final

(Bm)　(A)　(D/G)　　(G)　(D/A)　　　　(A)　　　(D)　(Dsus4)　(D)
Dm　　C　　F/B♭　　B♭　　F/C　　　　　C　　　F　　Fsus4　F (let ring)　*Fine*

God, _____　　　bathed in ___ the glo - ry of God! _____

VERSES

(B/D♯)　　　　(Em)　　(A/C♯)　　　　(A)　　　(F♯7)
D/F♯　　　　　Gm　　C/E　　　　　　C　　　A7

mf

1. Foun - tain of mer - cy,　grace flow - ing free,　streams of sal -
2. Here there is ha - ven,　heal - ing and health,　joy for the
3. Bread for our jour - ney　God will pro - vide.　Hope for all
4. Dark - ness is ban - ished,　night turned a - way.　Christ is our

(Bm)　　　(C)　　　　(Em)　　(A7sus4)　　　(A)　(Bm)　(A/C♯)
Dm　　　Eb　　　　Gm　　　C7sus4　　　C　　Dm　　C/E

poco rit.　　　　　　　　　　*rit.*　　*accel.*　　　*D.S.*

1. va - tion,　spill - ing with love from a tree! _____
2. ask - ing,　love in a - bun - dance of wealth! _____
3. a - ges,　Je - sus, com - pan - ion and guide! _____
4. sun - light,　lift - ing and lead - ing our way! _____

136 Somos el Cuerpo de Cristo/ We Are the Body of Christ

Jaime Cortez and Bob Hurd

Jaime Cortez

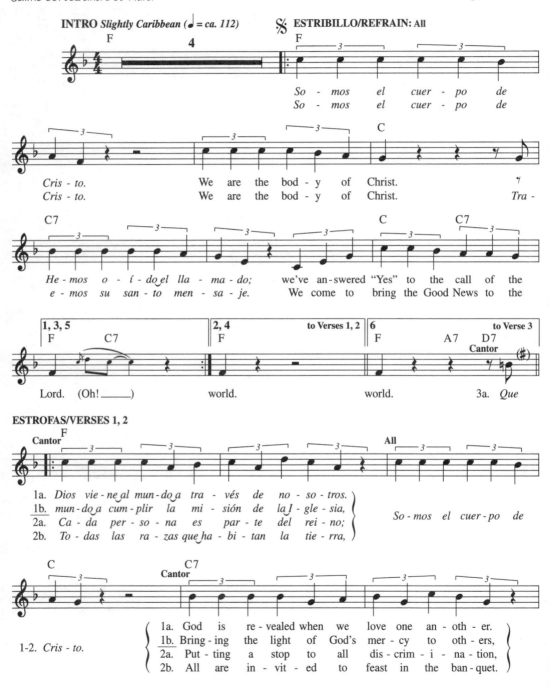

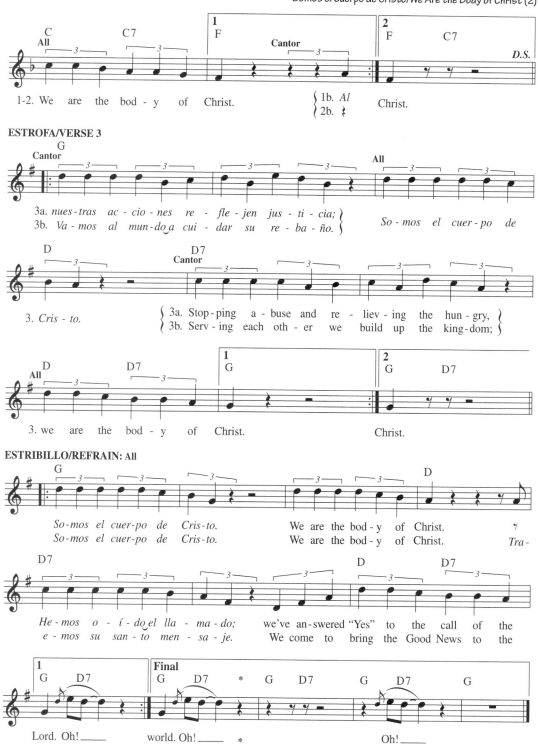

ESTROFA/VERSE 3

ESTRIBILLO/REFRAIN: All

*Entire final Refrain may be repeated from here.

137

The Summons

KELVINGROVE
Scottish Traditional Tune
Arranged by Bobby Fisher

John L. Bell

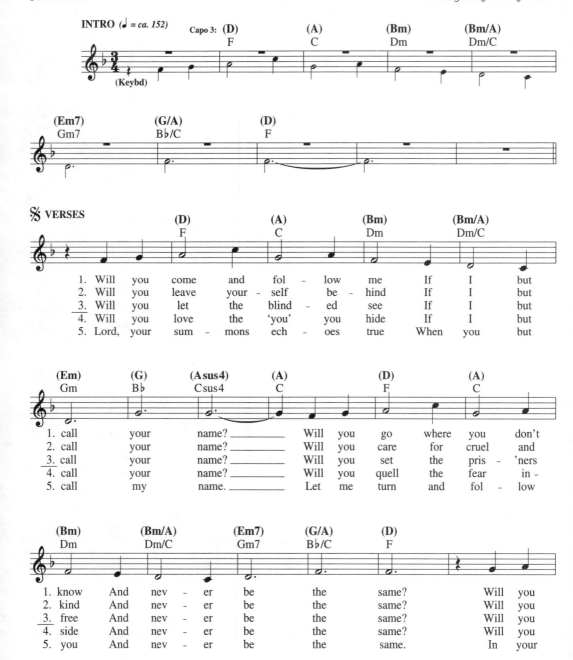

INTRO (♩ = ca. 152) Capo 3: (D) (A) (Bm) (Bm/A)
F C Dm Dm/C
(Keybd)

(Em7) (G/A) (D)
Gm7 B♭/C F

%% VERSES (D) (A) (Bm) (Bm/A)
F C Dm Dm/C

1. Will you come and fol - low me If I but
2. Will you leave your - self be - hind If I but
3. Will you let the blind - ed see If I but
4. Will you love the 'you' you hide If I but
5. Lord, your sum - mons ech - oes true When you but

(Em) (G) (Asus4) (A) (D) (A)
Gm B♭ Csus4 C F C

1. call your name? _____ Will you go where you don't
2. call your name? _____ Will you care for cruel and
3. call your name? _____ Will you set the pris - 'ners
4. call your name? _____ Will you quell the fear in -
5. call my name. _____ Let me turn and fol - low

(Bm) (Bm/A) (Em7) (G/A) (D)
Dm Dm/C Gm7 B♭/C F

1. know And nev - er be the same? Will you
2. kind And nev - er be the same? Will you
3. free And nev - er be the same? Will you
4. side And nev - er be the same? Will you
5. you And nev - er be the same. In your

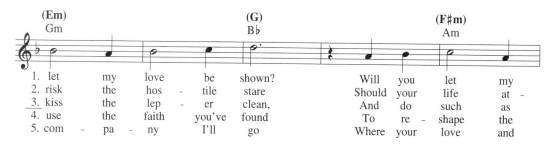

1. let my love be shown? Will you let my
2. risk the hos – tile stare Should your life at –
3. kiss the lep – er clean, And do such as
4. use the faith you've found To re – shape the
5. com – pa – ny I'll go Where your love and

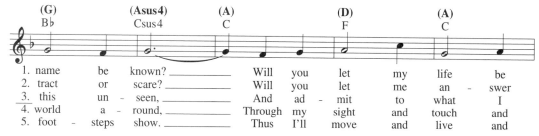

1. name be known? _____ Will you let my life be
2. tract or scare? _____ Will you let me an – swer
3. this un – seen, _____ And ad – mit to what I
4. world a – round, _____ Through my sight and touch and
5. foot – steps show. _____ Thus I'll move and live and

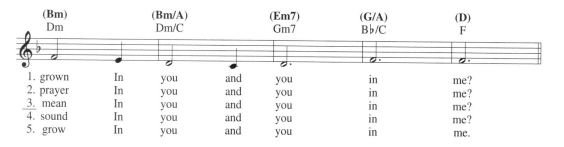

1. grown In you and you in me?
2. prayer In you and you in me?
3. mean In you and you in me?
4. sound In you and you in me?
5. grow In you and you in me.

INTERLUDE/CODA

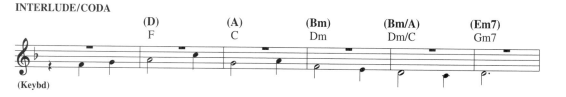

(Keybd)

138 Voice of Christ

Based on Luke 12:22–40;
Psalm 41:2–3; 72:12–13

Timothy R. Smith

VERSE 3

(Em7) F#m7   (F#7) G#7   (Bm) (Bm/A) C#m C#m/B   (G) A   (D/F#) E/G#   (A/E) B/F#

mp

3. The Lord hears the cry of the poor; ____ the lives of the weak he shall save.

(Em7) F#m7   (F#7) G#7   (Bm) (Bm/A) C#m C#m/B   (Em) F#m   (Em/G) F#m/A   (F#sus4) G#sus4   (F#) G#

cresc.

3. Bless-ed those who care for the poor; ____ hap-pi-ness is their re - ward. ____

𝄋 REFRAIN

(Bm) C#m   (D/F#) E/G#   (G) A   (Em7) F#m7   (A) B   (D/F#) E/G#   (G) A   (D/F#) E/G#   (Asus4) Bsus4   (A) B

f

We the hands, we the eyes, we the voice of Christ. ____

(D) E   (G/B) A/C#   (G) A   (Dmaj7/F#) Emaj7/G#   (Em7) F#m7   (Asus4) Bsus4   **1** (D) E   **Final** (D) E

rit. last time   *dim.* to Verse 4   *Fine*

O faith - ful ___ God, we en-trust our trea-sure to your heart.   heart.

VERSE 4

(D) E   *mp* (G/D) A/E   (G) A   (D/F#) E/G#   (Em7) F#m7

4. We a - wait ____ you with watch - ful ____ eyes, our lamps burn -

(G) A   (Asus4) Bsus4   (A) B   (D) E   (G/D) A/E

4. - ing bright. _____ Though we know ___ not when

(G) A   (D/F#) E/G#   (C/E) D/F#   (C) D   (Asus4) Bsus4   (A) B

cresc.   D.S.

4. you will re - turn, we stand wake - ful _____ through the night. _____

We Are Called to Serve

Julie and Tim Smith

REFRAIN

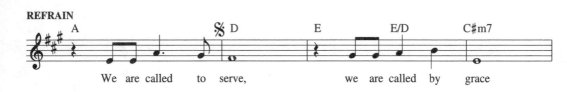

We are called to serve, we are called by grace

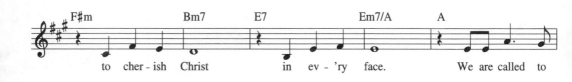

to cher-ish Christ in ev-'ry face. We are called to

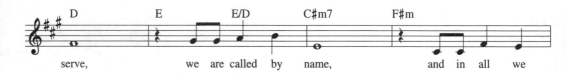

serve, we are called by name, and in all we

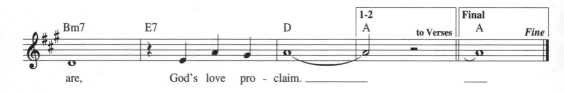

are, God's love pro-claim.

VERSES

1. Called be - yond our hu - man un - der - stand - ing, _____
2. Called to be a light a - mid the dark - ness, _____

1. called be - fore the world came in - to view.
2. called to help a doubt - ing world be - lieve.

With -
"Em -

1. in your moth - er's womb, _____ your name was known to me, for ___
2. pow - ered by my Spir - it, a - noint - ed with my love, you are

1. you did not ___ choose me, ___ no, I chose you. _____
2. called to give ___ and share ___ what you be - lieve." _____

} We are called to

140   We Are God's Work of Art

Mark Friedman

We Are the Light

141

Jesse Manibusan

Gathering & Sending Songs

142

We Are Marching
Siyahamba

South African

Melody: We are march - ing in the light of God, we are
Si - ya - hamb' e - ku - kha - nyen' kwen - khos', si - ya -

march-ing in the light of God. We are march - ing in the
hamb' e - ku - kha - nyen' kwen - khos'. Si - ya - hamb' e - ku - kha -

light of God, we are march-ing in the light of God.
nyen' kwen - khos', si - ya - hamb' e - ku - kha - nyen' kwen - khos'.

light of, the light of God.
- nyen' kwen, kha - nyen' kwen - khos'.

We are march-ing, Oo we are
Si - ya - ham - ba, Oo si - ya -

We are march-ing, march-ing, we are march-ing, march-ing, we are
Si - ya - ham - ba, ham - ba, si - ya - ham - ba, ham - ba, si - ya -

143   We Are the Light of the World

Jean Anthony Greif
Arranged by Tom Tomaszek

Based on the Beatitudes

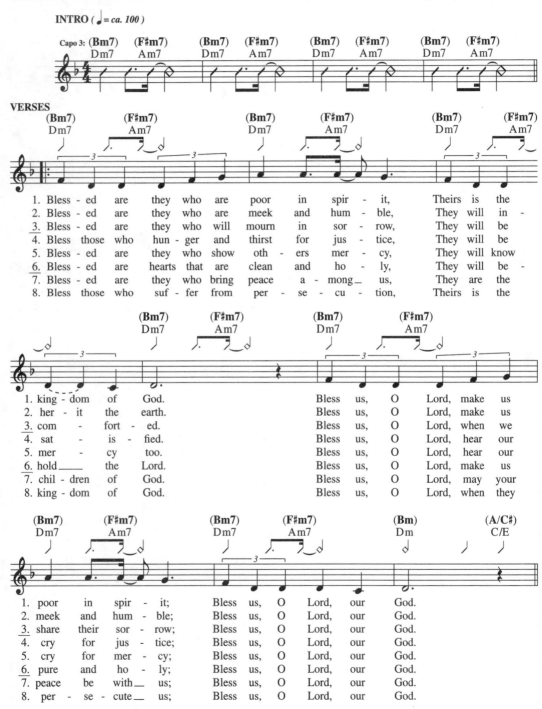

INTRO (♩ = ca. 100)

1. Bless - ed are they who are poor in spir - it, Theirs is the
2. Bless - ed are they who are meek and hum - ble, They will in -
3. Bless - ed are they who will mourn in sor - row, They will be
4. Bless those who hun - ger and thirst for jus - tice, They will be
5. Bless - ed are they who show oth - ers mer - cy, They will know
6. Bless - ed are they who hearts that are clean and ho - ly, They will be -
7. Bless - ed are they who bring peace a - mong us, They are the
8. Bless those who suf - fer from per - se - cu - tion, Theirs is the

1. king - dom of God. Bless us, O Lord, make us
2. her - it the earth. Bless us, O Lord, make us
3. com - fort - ed. Bless us, O Lord, when we
4. sat - is - fied. Bless us, O Lord, hear our
5. mer - cy too. Bless us, O Lord, hear our
6. hold the Lord. Bless us, O Lord, make us
7. chil - dren of God. Bless us, O Lord, may your
8. king - dom of God. Bless us, O Lord, when they

1. poor in spir - it; Bless us, O Lord, our God.
2. meek and hum - ble; Bless us, O Lord, our God.
3. share their sor - row; Bless us, O Lord, our God.
4. cry for jus - tice; Bless us, O Lord, our God.
5. cry for mer - cy; Bless us, O Lord, our God.
6. pure and ho - ly; Bless us, O Lord, our God.
7. peace be with us; Bless us, O Lord, our God.
8. per - se - cute us; Bless us, O Lord, our God.

287

144 We Gotta Love

Tom Booth, Israel Houghton and Matt Maher

145 We Will Serve the Lord

Suggested by Joshua 24:15

Rory Cooney

146 What Is Our Service to Be

Delores Dufner, OSB

Scot Crandal

293

147 With One Voice

Ricky Manalo

INTRO *With pride* (♩ = ca. 88)

Capo 1: **(D)** **(A/D)** **(G/D)** **(A)** **(G/B)** **(A/C♯)** **(D)** **(A/C♯)**
Eb Bb/Eb Ab/Eb Bb Ab/C Bb/D Eb Bb/D

mf

𝄋 VERSES

(G/B) **(A)** **(G/B)** **(A/C♯)** **(D)** **(A/D)** **(G/D)** **(D)**
Ab/C Bb Ab/C Bb/D Eb Bb/Eb Ab/Eb Eb

mf

1. Take the Word __ and go out __ to ev - 'ry land: __
2. Take the Word __ to our neigh - bor-hoods _ and streets: __
3. Take the Word __ to the peo - ple in __ de - spair: __
4. Take the Word __ to the na - tions ev - 'ry - where: __

(D/F♯) **(G add9)** **(A sus4)** **(A)**
Eb/G Ab add9 Bb sus4 Bb

1. shine the light of Christ for all __ to see! ____ May the
2. shine the light of Christ for all __ to see! ____ May we
3. shine the light of Christ for all __ to see! ____ May our
4. shine the light of Christ for all __ to see! ____ May the

(F♯m) **(Bm)** **(F♯)** **(F♯7/A♯)** **(Bm)**
Gm Cm G G7/B Cm

1. lives of those __ we touch __ sing praise to God a - bove. __ Let us
2. all set out __ to live __ in peace and har - mo - ny. __ They will
3. ac - tions and __ our deeds __ bring com - fort to their needs. __ And they'll
4. wit - ness of __ our lives __ trans - form the world a - new. __ And we'll

REFRAIN

(Em11) **(D/F♯)** **(G add9)** **(A)** **(G/A)** **(D)**
Fm11 Eb/G Ab add9 Bb Ab/Bb Eb

f

1. sing, ____ we'll sing: ____
2. see ____ and sing: ____
3. know ____ and sing: ____ With one voice we'll
4. shine, ____ we'll shine: ____

(Em7) **(A sus4)** **(A)** **(G/A)** **(D)** **(Em7)**
Fm7 Bb sus4 Bb Ab/Bb Eb Fm7

pass the Word _ a - long; ____ with one voice, bring jus - tice to __ the world. __

Gathering & Sending Songs

148 Witnesses

Paul Hillebrand

INTRO (♩ = ca. 152)

REFRAIN: All

We will be __ your wit - ness - es __ to all ___ the world. We will be __ your wit - ness - es __ to

to Optional Final Refrain

1 all __ the world. *D.S.*
2 all __ the world. to Verses
Simple Final Ending all __ the world. *Fine*

VERSES

Cantor / All / Cantor

1. Make dis - ci - ples, ___ make dis - ci - ples ___ of
2. Spread the news, ___ spread the news ___ a -
3. Thank the Lord, ___ thank the Lord ___ for

All

1. ev - 'ry - one __ we meet, __ of ev - 'ry - one __ we meet. __
2. cross ___ the land, __ a - cross ___ the land. __
3. gath - er - ing __ us here, __ for gath - er - ing __ us here. __

Cantor / All / Cantor / All / Cantor

1. You have called, __ you have called ___ us to be, __ us to be ___
2. You have come, __ you have come __ to give to us, __ to give to us ___
3. We will be, __ we will be __ your wit - ness - es, __ your wit - ness - es __ to

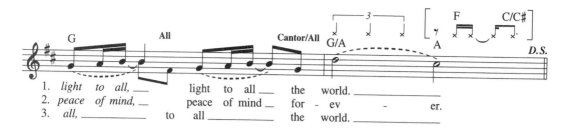

1. *light to all, __ light to all __ the world. _____*
2. *peace of mind, __ peace of mind __ for - ev - er.*
3. *all, _____ to all _____ the world. _____*

⊕ **OPTIONAL FINAL REFRAIN** (with modulation)

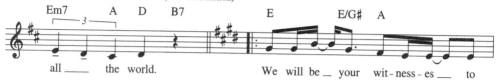

all ____ the world. We will be __ your wit - ness - es __ to

all ____ the world. We will be __ your wit - ness - es __ to

all ____ the world. all ____ the world.

COMMUNION SONGS

149   As One Unknown

Verses: Timothy Dudley-Smith
Refrain: Cyprian Consiglio

Verses: REPTON 8 6 88 6, alt
Charles H. Parry, 1848–1918
Arranged by Cyprian Consiglio
Refrain: Cyprian Consiglio

INTRO (♩ = ca. 102)

D   G   G/A A7 D   D   G   Asus4 A Bm7

%S VERSES

1. He comes to us — as — one un-known, a
2. He comes when souls — in — si - lence lie and
3. He comes to us — in — sound of seas, the
4. He comes in love — as — once he came by
5. He comes in truth — when — faith is grown; be-

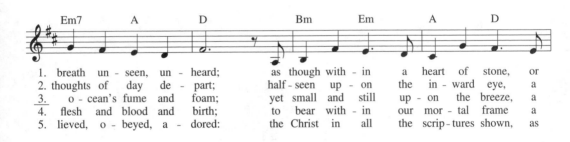

Em7   A   D   Bm   Em   A   D

1. breath un - seen, un - heard;   as though with - in a heart of stone, or
2. thoughts of day de - part;   half - seen up - on the in - ward eye, a
3. o - cean's fume and foam;   yet small and still up - on the breeze, a
4. flesh and blood and birth;   to bear with - in our mor - tal frame a
5. lieved, o - beyed, a - dored: the Christ in all the scrip - tures shown, as

Bm   G   Em   Asus4 A7   D/F♯   G   Asus4 A

1. shriv - eled seed in dark - ness — sown, a — pulse of be - ing — stirred. ___
2. fall - ing star a - cross the — sky of — night with - in — the — heart. ___
3. wind that stirs the tops of — trees, a — voice to call — us — home. ___
4. life, a death, a sav - ing — name, for — ev - 'ry child — of — earth. ___
5. yet un - seen, but not un - known, our — Sav - ior and — our — Lord. ___

REFRAIN

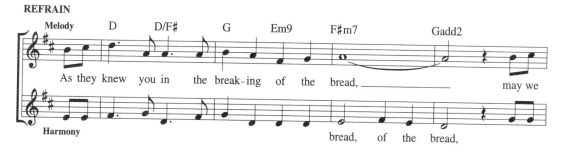

As they knew you in the break-ing of the bread, _____ may we
bread, of the bread,

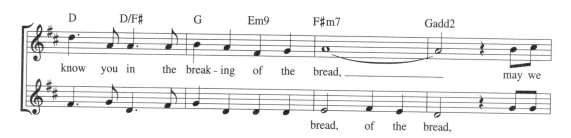

know you in the break-ing of the bread, _____ may we
bread, of the bread,

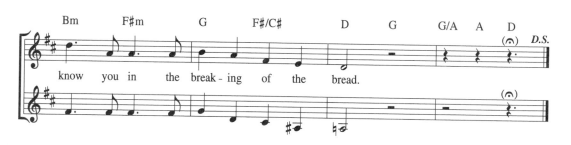

know you in the break-ing of the bread.

150 Bread of Life

Bobby Fisher

INTRO *Gently, reverently* (♩ = ca. 80)

1. Bread of life and cup of hope, we come as gift to you.
2. Lov-ing Lord, Cre - a - tor God, o - pen our eyes to see

1. Change our hearts; fill us with peace. Trans-form our lives a - new.
2. the good that lives in each of us, that called the world to be.

1. O - pen our eyes so that we might see your pres - ence in one an - oth - er.
2. And when we fail to __ see the good, when friend-ships fal - ter and crum-ble,

1. Your life, poured out in love to - day, u - nites us all in you.
2. give us the cour - age to for-give that we may live in peace.

INTERLUDE

VERSE 3

3. Liv-ing Word, O Son of God, your love shows us the way

3. that we may live in har - mo-ny, and from you nev - er stray.

3. Wipe all op-pres-sion __ from our midst; give us a love for all peo - ple.

3. Your song of jus - tice sing in us, to live for peace to - day.

151 Come to the Lord

Steve Angrisano and Tom Tomaszek

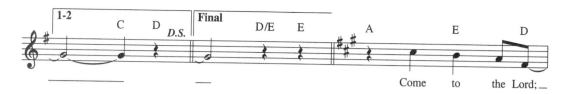

Come to the Lord; —

come to the ta - ble of last - ing life. — Bring your bur -

- dens; _____ there's _ no price, _____ just Come to the Lord. _

Come to the Lord. _____

152

Here I Am, Lord

Dan Schutte

153   I Am the Bread of Life

John Michael Talbot
Harmony by Phil Perkins

Based on John 6:35–58

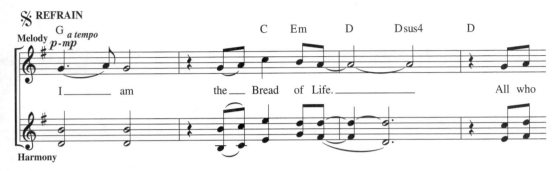

I am the Bread of Life. All who

eat this Bread will nev - er die.

I am God's love re - vealed. I am

bro - ken that you might be healed.

154 I Know That My Redeemer Lives

Based on Job 19, Psalm 27, Isaiah 25

Scott Soper

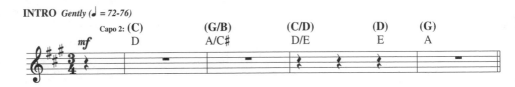

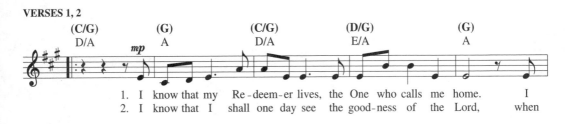

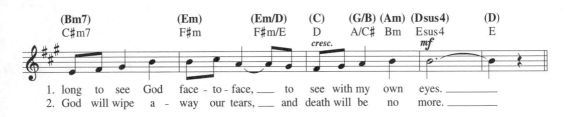

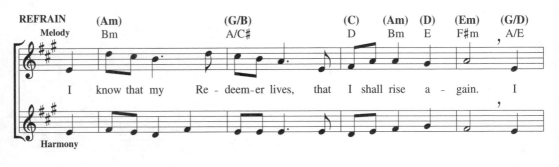

1. I know that my Re-deem-er lives, the One who calls me home. I
2. I know that I shall one day see the good-ness of the Lord, when

1. long to see God face - to - face, ___ to see with my own eyes. ___
2. God will wipe a - way our tears, ___ and death will be no more. ___

REFRAIN

I know that my Re - deem-er lives, that I shall rise a - gain. I

know that my Re - deem-er lives, that I shall rise a - gain.

VERSE 3

3. The last day I shall rise a - gain, shall be re-made like God. My

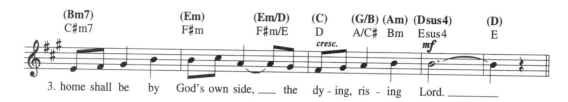

3. home shall be by God's own side, ___ the dy - ing, ris - ing Lord. _____

FINAL REFRAIN

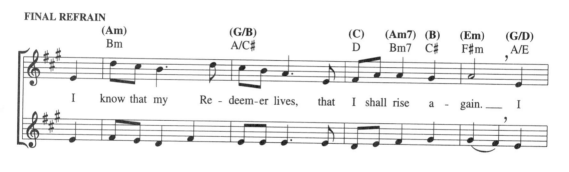

I know that my Re - deem-er lives, that I shall rise a - gain. ___ I

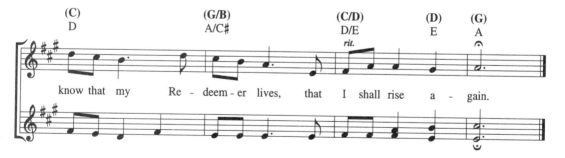

know that my Re - deem - er lives, that I shall rise a - gain.

155 Lead Us to Your Table

Tom Tomaszek

Tom Tomaszek and Steve Angrisano

Lead us to your ta - ble, feed___ us for the jour - ney, bind___ us all to - geth - er for___

___ the sac - ri - fice. Lead us to com-mun - ion, be___ our hope and vis - ion; we___

___ will be your pres-ence in___ the world to - day.___ We are

one___ in your love.___ We are one___

___ in your love.___ We are one___ in your love.___

We are one___ in your love.___ We are

Final

___ We are one___ in your love.___

156

Like the Bread

Tom Booth
T. Timothy Casey

Tom Booth

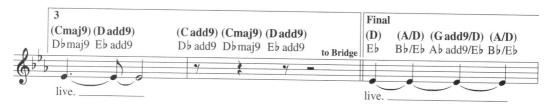

3
| (Cmaj9) (Dadd9) | (Cadd9) (Cmaj9) (Dadd9) | **Final** (D) (A/D) (Gadd9/D) (A/D) |
| D♭maj9 E♭add9 | D♭add9 D♭maj9 E♭add9   to Bridge | E♭   B♭/E♭ A♭add9/E♭ B♭/E♭ |

live. ____

live. ____

| (D) (A/D) (Gadd9/D) (A/D) | (D) (A/D) (Gadd9/D) (A/D) | |
| E♭ B♭/E♭ A♭add9/E♭ B♭/E♭ | E♭ B♭/E♭ A♭add9/E♭ B♭/E♭ | *Fine* |

VERSE 1

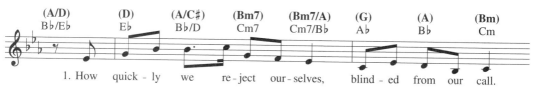

| (A/D) | (D) | (A/C♯) | (Bm7) | (Bm7/A) | (G) | (A) | (Bm) |
| B♭/E♭ | E♭ | B♭/D | Cm7 | Cm7/B♭ | A♭ | B♭ | Cm |

1. How quick - ly we re - ject our - selves, blind - ed from our call.

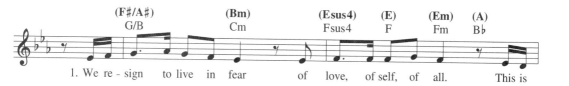

| (F♯/A♯) | (Bm) | (Esus4) | (E) | (Em) | (A) |
| G/B | Cm | Fsus4 | F | Fm | B♭ |

1. We re - sign to live in fear of love, of self, of all. This is

| (G) | (A) | (Bm) | (F♯/A♯) | (F♯) | (Gmaj7) |
| A♭ | B♭ | Cm | G/B | G | A♭maj7 |

1. not the will of God, for the cho - sen must be free. We are

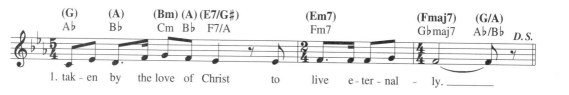

| (G) | (A) | (Bm) (A) (E7/G♯) | (Em7) | (Fmaj7) | (G/A) |
| A♭ | B♭ | Cm B♭ F7/A | Fm7 | G♭maj7 | A♭/B♭ *D.S.* |

1. tak - en by the love of Christ to live e - ter - nal - ly. ____

313

VERSE 2

BRIDGE

Bread for the World

157

Bernadette Farrell

INTRO (♩ = ca. 58)

(tacet)   A   Bm   Esus4   E

(Keybd)

REFRAIN

A   D/A   E/A   Asus4   A   C#m   D

Bread for the world: a world of hun - ger.   Wine for all peo - ples:

Esus4   E   Asus4   A   C#m   D/F#   Esus4   E   Asus4   A

peo - ple who thirst. ___   May we who eat   be bread for oth - ers.

C#m   Dadd9   D

1-3 Esus4   E   Asus4   A   *to Verses*

Final Esus4   E   Asus4   A   *Fine*

May we who drink ___ pour out our love. _____ pour out our love. _____

VERSES

A   D/A   A   E/G#   F#m7

1. Lord Je - sus Christ, you are the bread of life, ___ bro - ken to reach and
2. Lord Je - sus Christ, you are the wine of peace, ___ poured in - to hearts once
3. Lord Je - sus Christ, you call us to your feast, ___ at which the rich and

Bm7   Esus4   E   D   F#m

1. heal the wounds of hu - man pain. ___ Where we di - vide your peo - ple, you are
2. bro - ken and where dry-ness sleeps. ___ Where we are tired and wea - ry, you are
3. pow'r-ful have be - come the least. ___ Where we sur - vive on oth - ers in our

Bm   E/G#   E   A   Bm7   Esus4   E

D.S.

1. wait - ing there ___ on bend - ed knee to wash our feet with end - less care. ___
2. wait - ing there ___ to be the way which beck-ons us be - yond de - spair. ___
3. hu - man greed, ___ you walk a - mong us beg-ging for your ev - 'ry need. ___

Communion Songs

158

Now We Remain

1 Corinthians 1; 1 John; 2 Timothy

David Haas

1. Once we were peo-ple a-fraid, lost in the night. ___ Then by your
1. cross we were saved; ___ Dead be-came liv-ing, life from your giv-ing. ___

VERSE 2

2. Some-thing which we have known, some-thing we've touched, _____ what we have

2. seen with our eyes: _____ This we have heard; life giv-ing word. _____

VERSE 3

3. He chose to give of him-self, be-came our bread. _____ Bro-ken,

3. that we might live. _____ Love be-yond love, pain for our pain. _____

VERSE 4

4. We are the pres-ence of God; this is our call. _____

4. Now to be-come bread and wine: _____ Food for the hun-gry, life for the

4. wea-ry, _____ for to live with the Lord, we must die with the Lord. _____

159 O Taste and See

Psalm 34:2–9, 11–13, 19

Marty Haugen

VERSE 2

2. For God has heard ___ my an - guished cries, and de - liv - ered me

2. from all my foes. ___ O look to God ___ that you might shine, ___

2. ___ your fac - es be ra - diant with joy. ___

VERSE 3

3. When the poor cry out, ___ God hears and saves them, res - cues them

3. from their dis - tress. ___ God's an - gel watch - es near to those ___

3. ___ who look to their God to save them. ___

VERSE 4

4. O taste and see ___ that God is good, how hap - py the

4. ones who find ref - uge. ___ The might-y shall ___ grow weak and hun -

4. - gry, those who seek God lack noth - ing. ___

319

VERSE 5

5. Come, my chil - dren, hear me, _____ I will teach you the

5. fear of God. _____ Come, all of you _____ who thirst for life _____

5. _____ and seek joy in all of your days. _____

VERSE 6

6. For God is close _____ to the bro - ken - heart - ed, near to those

6. crushed in spir - it. _____ The hand of God _____ re - deems your life, _

6. _ a ref - uge for all those who seek. _____

Seek Ye First

160

Based on Matthew 6:33; 7:7; 4:4

Karen Lafferty

*Parts 1 and 2 may be sung separately or together.

Communion Songs

161 One Bread, One Body

Based on 1 Corinthians 10:16, 17; 12:4;
Galatians 3:28; The Didache 9

John Foley, S.J.

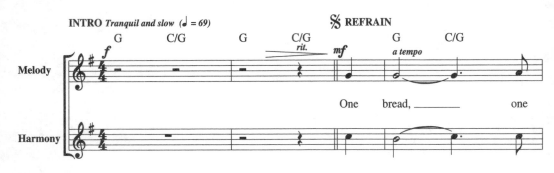

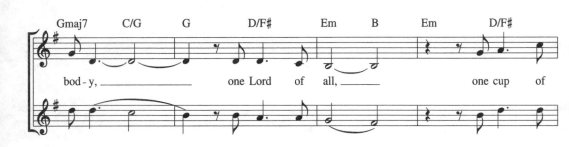

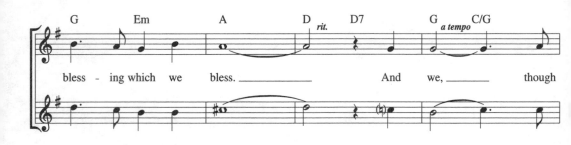

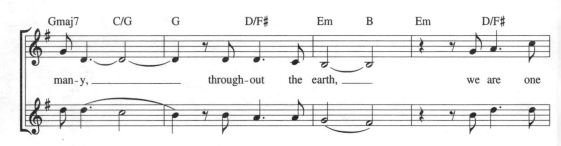

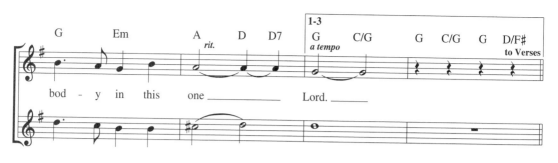

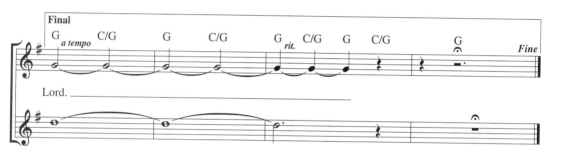

VERSES *Slightly faster, with excitement ($\quarternote$ = 72)*

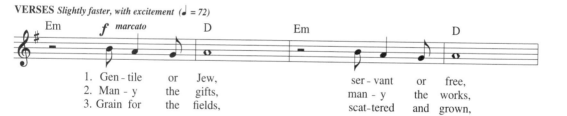

1. Gen-tile or Jew, ser-vant or free,
2. Man-y the gifts, man-y the works,
3. Grain for the fields, scat-tered and grown,

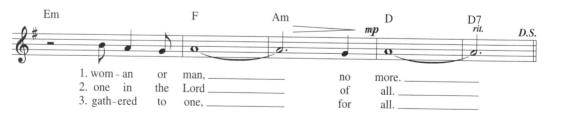

1. wom-an or man, _____ no more. _____
2. one in the Lord _____ of all. _____
3. gath-ered to one, _____ for all. _____

162

Pescador de Hombres/
Lord, You Have Come

Spanish text: Cesáreo Gabaráin
English text: Robert C. Trupia

Cesáreo Gabaráin

ESTRIBILLO/REFRAIN

Se - ñor, _____ me has mi - ra-do a los o - jos, _____
O Lord, _____ with your eyes set up - on me, _____

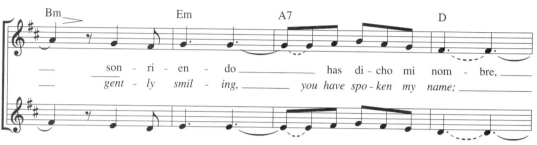

__ son - ri - en - do _____ has di - cho mi nom - bre, _____
__ gent - ly smil - ing, _____ you have spo - ken my name; _____

__ en la a - re - na _____ he de - ja - do mi bar - ca, _____
__ all I longed for _____ I have found by the wa - ter, _____

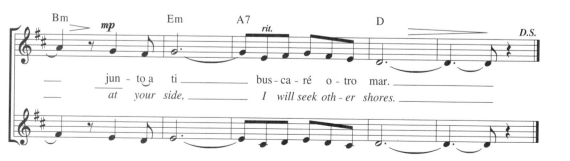

__ jun - to a ti _____ bus - ca - ré o - tro mar. _____
__ at your side, _____ I will seek oth - er shores. _____

163 Table of Plenty

Dan Schutte

INTRO *Lively (♩ = 152)*

REFRAIN

Melody

Come to the feast ___ of heav - en and earth! Come to the ta -

Harmony

Let us come to the feast! O come to the ta -

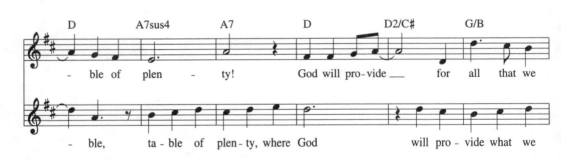

- ble of plen - ty! God will pro-vide ___ for all that we

- ble, ta - ble of plen - ty, where God will pro - vide what we

1-4

need, here at the ta - ble of plen - ty. ___

need, here at the ta - ble of plen - ty. ___

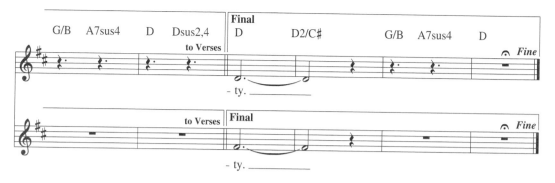

VERSES

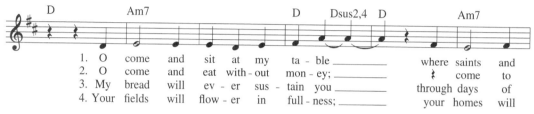

1. O come and sit at my ta - ble _____ where saints and
2. O come and eat with - out mon - ey; _____ come to
3. My bread will ev - er sus - tain you _____ through days of
4. Your fields will flow - er in full - ness; _____ your homes will

1. sin - ners are friends. _____ I wait to wel - come the lost and
2. drink with - out price. _____ My feast of glad - ness will feed your
3. sor - row and woe. _____ My wine will flow like a sea of
4. flour - ish in peace. _____ For I, the giv - er of home and

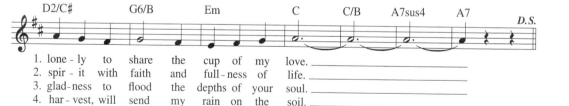

1. lone - ly to share the cup of my love. _____
2. spir - it with faith and full - ness of life. _____
3. glad - ness to flood the depths of your soul. _____
4. har - vest, will send my rain on the soil. _____

164

Ven al Banquete/
Come to the Feast

Bob Hurd, Pia Moriarty and Jaime Cortez

Bob Hurd

ESTRIBILLO/REFRAIN (♩ = ca. 156)

(Bilingual) Ven, ven al ban - que - te. Ven a la
(Español) Ven, ven al ban - que - te. Ven a la
(English) Come, come to the ban - quet. Come, _____

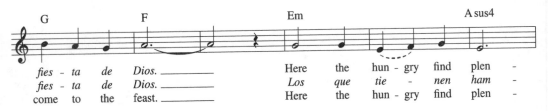

fies - ta de Dios. _____ Here the hun - gry find plen -
fies - ta de Dios. _____ Los que tie - nen ham -
come to the feast. _____ Here the hun - gry find plen -

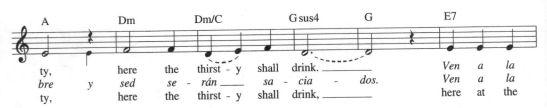

ty, here the thirst - y shall drink. _____ Ven a la
bre y sed se - rán sa - cia - dos. Ven a la
ty, here the thirst - y shall drink, _____ here at the

1-6

ce - na de Cris - to, come _____ to _____ the feast. _____
ce - na de Cris - to, ven a la fies - ta de Dios. _____
sup - per of Je - sus, come _____ to _____ the feast. _____

to Verses

Final

feast, _____ come _____ to _____ the feast. _____
Dios, _____ ven a la fies - ta de Dios. _____
feast, _____ come _____ to _____ the feast. _____

Fine

Play Refrain as an Intro.

ESTROFAS/VERSES

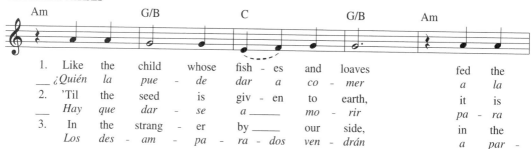

1. Like the child whose fish - es and loaves fed the
___ *¿Quién la pue - de dar a co - mer a la*
2. 'Til the seed is giv - en to earth, it is
___ *Hay que dar - se a _____ mo - rir pa - ra*
3. In the strang - er by _____ our side, in the
Los des - am - pa - ra - dos ven - drán a par -

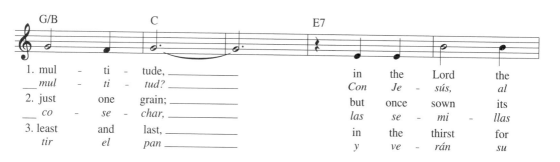

1. mul - ti - tude, _____ in the Lord the
___ *mul - ti - tud? _____ Con Je - sús, al*
2. just one grain; _____ but once sown its
___ *co - se - char, _____ las se - mi - llas*
3. least and last, _____ in the thirst for
tir el pan _____ y ve - rán su

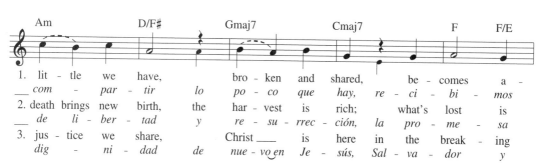

1. lit - tle we have, bro - ken and shared, be - comes a -
___ *com - par - tir lo po - co que hay, re - ci - bi - mos*
2. death brings new birth, the har - vest is rich; what's lost is
___ *de li - ber - tad y re - su - rrec - ción, la pro - me - sa*
3. jus - tice we share, Christ ___ is here in the break - ing
dig - ni - dad de nue - vo en Je - sús, Sal - va - dor y

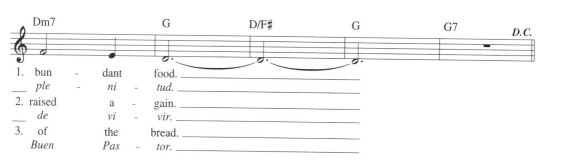

1. bun - dant food. _____
___ *ple - ni - tud. _____*
2. raised a - gain. _____
___ *de vi - vir. _____*
3. of the bread. _____
Buen Pas - tor. _____

329

165
We Are One Body

Dana Scallon
Arranged by Gerry Brown; transcribed by S. Beddia

INTRO

REFRAIN 1

We are one bod - y, ___ one bod - y in Christ; ___ and we do not stand a-

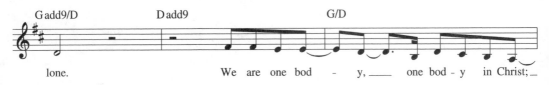

lone. We are one bod - y, ___ one bod - y in Christ;

and he came that we might have life. ___ For he tells us

VERSES 1, 2

1. When you eat my bod - y and you drink my blood, I will live in you ___
2. Can you hear them cry - ing, can you feel their pain? Will you feed my hun -

1. ___ and you will live in my love. When you eat my bod - y and you drink my
2. - gry, will you help ___ my lame? See the un - born ba - by, the for - got - ten

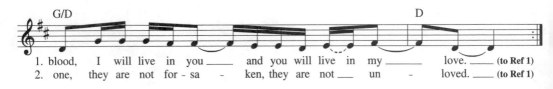

1. blood, I will live in you ___ and you will live in my ___ love. ___ **(to Ref 1)**
2. one, they are not for - sa - ken, they are not ___ un - loved. ___ **(to Ref 1)**

VERSE 3

3. I am the Way, the Truth, the Life, I am the Fi - nal Sac - ri - fice, I am the Way, the Truth, the

3. Life; he who be-lieves in me will have e - ter - nal life. I am the Way, the Truth, the

3. Life, I am the Fi - nal Sac - ri - fice, I am the Way, the Truth, the

3. Life; he who be-lieves in me will have e - ter - nal life.

VERSE 4

4. I have come, your Sav - ior, that you might have life, through the tears — and sor -

4. - row, through the toils and strife. Lis-ten when I call — you, for I know your

4. need, come to me, — your shep - herd, for my flock I feed. _____

REFRAIN 2

We are one bod - y, ___ one bod-y in Christ; ___ and we do not stand a-
lone. We are one bod - y, ___ one bod-y in Christ; ___
and he came that we might have life. ___

VERSE 5

5. At the name of Je - sus ev-'ry knee shall bend; Je-sus is ___ the Lord ___
5. ___ and he will come a - gain. At the name of Je - sus ev-'ry knee shall
5. bend; Je - sus is ___ the Lord ___ and he will come a - gain. _____ Yea!

REFRAIN 3

We are one bod - y, ___ one bod-y in Christ; ___ and we do not stand a - lone.
We are one bod - y, ___ one bod-y in Christ; ___ and he came that we might have life. ___

1
Bᵇ add9 to Verse 6

2
Bᵇ add9 Fadd9 *D.S.*

Final
Bᵇ add9 *mp* *rit.* F *Fine*

He came that we might have life.

VERSE 6

Fadd9

Bᵇ add9

6. On the rock of Pe - ter, see my Church I

Melody

Counter-Melody mf We are one bod - y; ____

Fadd9
6. build.

Bᵇ add9
Come re-ceive __ my spir - it, with my gifts be

and we do not stand a - lone.

Fadd9
6. filled.

Bᵇ add9
For you are my bod - y, you're my hands and

We are one bod - y; ____

Fadd9
6. feet. ____

Bᵇ add9
Speak my word __ of life __ to ev'ry one __ you meet.

Fadd9
D.S.

and he came that we might have life. __

166 Worthy Is the Lamb

Based on Revelation 5:9–14

Ricky Manalo

God. _____

God, the good - ness of God.

VERSES

1. Wor - thy are you, O Pas - chal Lamb. Wis - dom and
2. Wor - thy are you, O Bread of Life. Sal - va - tion and
3. Wor - thy are you, O Ris - en Christ. Won - ders and

1. strength be - long now to you. You laid down your
2. joy be - long now to us. By con - quer - ing
3. signs, re - veal - ing your might. Your pow - er and

1. life and died up - on the cross: we've be - come a
2. death and ris - ing to new life, we've be - come a
3. glo - ry shines up - on our lives: we've be - come a

1. peo - ple of hope. _____
2. peo - ple of praise. _____
3. light for the world. _____

335   *Communion Songs*

167 We Come Today

Mark Friedman

INTRO Gently (♩ = ca. 108)

(Keybd)

℅ REFRAIN

We come to-day to break this bread and share this cup of wine. We gath-er at your ta-ble now to hear your words of life. And though there are so man-y here to-day, we all are one: one fam-i-ly, one bod-y, and one Church;

1-4 we are your own.

Final we are your own.

VERSES

1. We thank you, God, for Je - sus, who calls us to this feast
2. We thank you for our par - ents who care for us each day,
3. We thank you for the peo - ple who teach us in your ways,
4. We thank you for cre - a - tion, the beau - ty of the earth;

1. to share in one com - mun - ion in your name.
2. the fam - 'ly gath - ered 'round us here in love.
3. who help us learn to love our neigh - bors well.
4. with grate - ful hearts we thank you for your gifts.

Cry the Gospel

168

Tom Booth

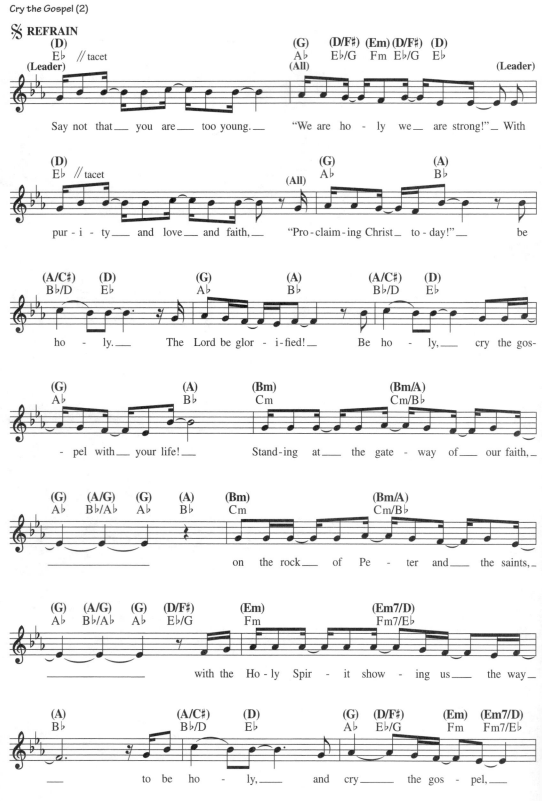

169

Awesome God

Rich Mullins
Arranged by Tom Booth

1. - turn is ver - y close and so you bet - ter be be - liev - in' that our
2. hope that we have___ not___ too___ quick - ly for - got - ten that our

REFRAIN

1. God is an awe - some God!
2. God is an awe - some God! } Our God is an awe - some God; he reigns from___

heav'n a - bove with wis - dom,___ pow'r and love. Our God is an awe - some God! Our

God is an awe - some God!

Final

God is an awe - some God! Our God is an awe - some God! Our God is an awe - some God!

170 Be Not Afraid

Based on Isaiah 43:2–3; Luke 6:20ff

Bob Dufford, SJ

171

Be With Me, Lord

Refrain: Traditional, Arranged by Tom Booth
Verses: Tom Booth

172 Behold the Cross

Based on the Liturgy for Good Friday

Bob Hurd
Harmony by Craig Kingsbury

INTRO (♩ = ca. 84)   VERSES 1-3

1. Be - hold the cross   on which was   hung
2. Nails in his hands,   nails in his   feet,
3. Eyes that won't see,   ears that won't   hear,

(Verse 3 harmony)

1. life's ver - y   Lord,_____   God's dar - ling   One;   Ma - ry's   own
2. a trai - tor   kiss_____   up - on_____   his   cheek;   and his pierced
3. lips that de - ny_____   the friend once   so   dear;   slow - ly   he

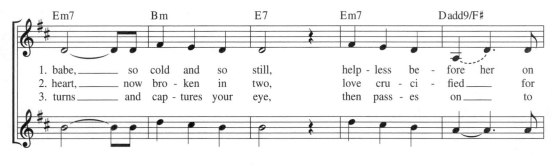

1. babe,_____   so cold and   so   still,   help - less be - fore her   on
2. heart,_____   now bro - ken   in   two,   love cru - ci - fied____   for
3. turns____   and cap - tures your   eye,   then pass - es   on____   to

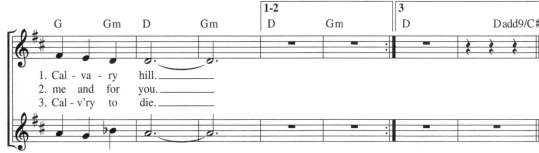

1-2   3

1. Cal - va - ry   hill._____
2. me and for   you._____
3. Cal - v'ry to   die.

VERSE 4

4. Be - hold the cross_____ of Christ in our midst:

4. all those who bear_____ his wounds in their flesh.

4. Suf - f'ring for crimes_____ of mer - cy and peace, signs of the

4. king - dom on Cal - va - ry street._____

VERSE 5

5. Be - hold the cross on which was hung life's ver - y Lord, God's dar - ling

5. One; Ma - ry's own babe,_____ so cold and so still, help - less be -

5. fore her on Cal - va - ry hill._____

173 Blessed Are They

Luke 11:28

Tom Tomaszek

Bless - ed __ are they who hear the Word __ of God and keep it;

bless - ed __ are they who hear the Word __ of God.

God, the Word of God.

Bless - ed __ are they who hear the Word __ of God and keep it; bless - ed __ are

Bless - ed __ are they. _____ Bless - ed __ are

174 Come, Lord Jesus

Verses based on a prayer ascribed to St. Francis

Steve Angrisano and Tom Tomaszek

VERSE 1

1. Where there's de - spair in life, ___ Lord, ___ let me be your voice ___

1. ___ of hope. _____ Where there's in - ju - ry, Lord, ___

1. ___ let me be ___ your voice of peace. _____

D.S.

VERSE 2

2. Where there is sad - ness let ___ me be ___ your com - fort and ___

2. ___ your joy. _____ When there's fear in our hearts ___

2. ___ let me be ___ a sign of faith. _____

D.S.

INTERLUDE

(Keybd)

D.S. al fine

175 Everybody Sing Alleluia

Tony & Lynn Melendez
Augie & Dawn Leal

Tony Melendez and Augie Leal

How Beautiful

176

Twila Paris

177 Fly Like a Bird

Based on Psalm 139

Ken Canedo

178 God's Eye Is on the Sparrow

Based on Job 11:16;
Matthew 6:25–34; John 14:18

Bob Hurd

INTRO/INTERLUDE (♩ = 63–66)

(Keybd)

VERSES

1. As the rain first falls and then,
2. Now your heart it feels like,

1. then it flows a - way,
2. like an o - pen wound;

1. first you'll feel and then for - get,
2. once so full of life and joy,

1. then for - get your pain.
2. now an emp - ty room.

179 He Is Exalted

Twila Paris

*Sing cue notes after the first time.

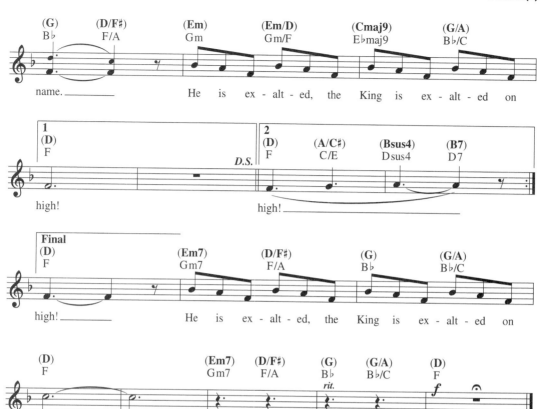

name. _____ He is ex - alt - ed, the King is ex - alt - ed on

1
(D)
F

high!

D.S.

2
(D)
F
(A/C♯)
C/E
(Bsus4)
Dsus4
(B7)
D7

high! _____

Final
(D)
F
(Em7)
Gm7
(D/F♯)
F/A
(G)
B♭
(G/A)
B♭/C

high! _____ He is ex - alt - ed, the King is ex - alt - ed on

(D)
F
(Em7)
Gm7
(D/F♯)
F/A
(G)
B♭
(G/A)
B♭/C
(D)
F

rit.

f

high! _____

Prayer & Praise Songs

180

Here I Am

Tom Booth

Here I am, stand-ing right be-

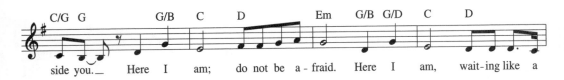

side you.__ Here I am; do not be a-fraid. Here I am, wait-ing like a

lov - er.__ I am here; here I am. _____ am. I am

here; here I am. _____

VERSE 1

1. Do not fear when the tempt - er calls you.__ Do not

Prayer & Praise Songs

181 Hope to Carry On

Rich Mullins

INTRO (♩= ca. 96)

1. I can see
2. (I can hear)
3. (You___ know)

VERSES

1. Je - sus   hang - ing on the cross,   I can see
2. Je - sus   say - ing, "Fa - ther for - give."___   I can hear
3. Pe - ter   put a - way his sword.   I can see

1. Je - sus   hang - ing on the cross,___   I can see
2. Je - sus   say - ing, "Fa - ther for - give."___   I can hear
3. Pe - ter   put - ting a - way___ his sword.___   I can see

1. Je - sus   hang - ing on the cross. He came look - ing for the lost.___
2. Je - sus   say - ing, "Fa - ther for - give."___ What a thing___ he___ did.___
3. Pe - ter,   he put a - way his sword. He won't fight___ no___ more.___

REFRAIN

Love has___ come,___ love has___ come,___ love has___ come,___ and it's

giv - en me hope___ to car - ry on. ___

1. 2. I can hear

2. **BRIDGE**

I can see love; ___ love is

182

Humble Thyself

Bob Hudson

I Give You Permission

Tom Booth

184 I Could Sing of Your Love Forever

Martin Smith

O - ver the moun - tains and — the sea your riv - er runs — with love — for me,

and I will o - pen up — my heart — and let the Heal - er set — me free.

I'm hap - py to — be in — the truth, and I will dai - ly lift — my hands,

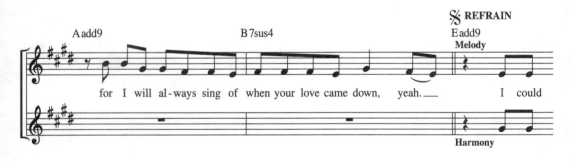

for I will al - ways sing of when your love came down, yeah. — I could

sing of your love — for - ev - er. I could sing of your love —

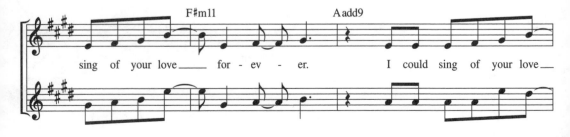

185

I See You

Rich Mullins

INTRO (♩ = ca. 80)

VERSES

1. Lord, you're lead - ing me
2. And you take my hand
3. And the ea - gle flies
4. Well, the grass will die

1. with a cloud by day, and then in the night, the glow of a
2. and you wash it clean. I know the prom - ised land is light - years a -
3. and the riv - ers run. I look through the night and I can see the
4. and the flow - ers fall, but your Word's a - live and will be

REFRAIN
Melody

1. burn - ing flame.
2. head of me.
3. ris - ing sun.
4. af - ter all.

And ev - 'ry-where I go I see you.   Ev-'ry-

Harmony

And ev-'ry-where I go I see you.

where I go I see you.   And ev-'ry-

1 | **D.S.** to Vs 2 | **2-4**

Ev-'ry-where I go I see you.   where I go I see you.

Prayer & Praise Songs

186 In the Light

Charlie Peacock

be my _ sal - va - tion, 'cause all I want _ is to _ be in _ the light.

All I want _ is to _ be in _ the light. _____

1
Em Bm7 Em Cmaj7 D Em

2
Em Bm7 Em

to Verse 2

Final
Em Bm7 Em Fine

I wan - na _____

VERSE 2

2. The dis-ease of _ self ____ runs through my _ blood, _ it's a can - cer fa - tal to _

2. _ my soul. _ Ev - 'ry at-tempt _ on my _ be - half has failed _ to

2. bring this sick-ness un - der _ con-trol. _____ Tell me, what's go-in' on in-side of me? _

2. I de - spise my own _ be-hav - ior. _ This on - ly serves _ to con-firm _

2. my sus - pi-cions that I'm still a man _ in need of a Sav - ior. _ I wan-na

187 Jesus Christ, Inner Light

Text suggested by
Brother Roger, Taizé Community

Suzanne Toolan, RSM

OPTIONAL INTRO (♩ = *ca. 60*)

(Instr. Solo)

𝄋 OSTINATO REFRAIN

Capo 2: (Am) (Am/G) (Fmaj7) (E) (Am/C)
Bm   Bm/A   Gmaj7   F#   Bm/D

Je - sus Christ, in - ner light, let not our own

VERSES: Cantor

1. Je - sus ___ Christ, source of light, in you we dis-

2. Ris - en Christ, you go down to the depths, to the depths of our

3. Je - sus ___ Christ, in our search for ___ you, bring us in-

4. Je - sus ___ Christ, help us to

188

Lean on Me

Bill Withers

Prayer & Praise Songs

189 Lord, I Lift Your Name on High

Rick Founds
Arranged by Ed Bolduc

INTRO (♩ = ca. 96)

Lord, I lift your name on high.
Lord, I love to sing your prais-es.
I'm so glad you're in my life.
I'm so glad you came to save us.
save us.

Melody: You came from heav-en to earth to show the way. From the earth
Harmony

190 My Heart Belongs to You

Tom Booth

INTRO (♩ = ca. 62)   VERSES 1, 2

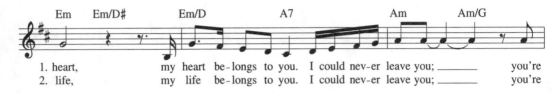

1. My heart, my heart be-longs to you. My
2. My life, my life be-longs to you. My

1. heart, my heart be-longs to you. I could nev-er leave you; _____ you're
2. life, my life be-longs to you. I could nev-er leave you; _____ you're

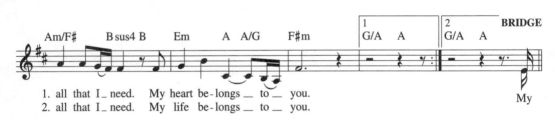

1. all that I _ need. My heart be-longs _ to _ you.
2. all that I _ need. My life be-longs _ to _ you.

BRIDGE

My

Melody

Lord and God, _ you've helped me _ to see that my life is found in your

Harmony

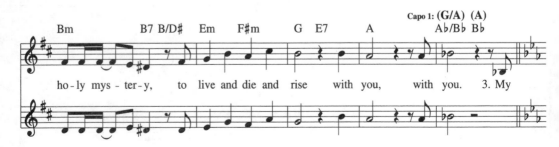

Capo 1: (G/A) (A)

ho-ly mys-ter-y, to live and die and rise with you, with you. 3. My

*Capo 1 begins at Verse 3.

VERSE 3

191 My Life Is in Your Hands

Kathy Troccoli

Kathy Troccoli
and Bill Montvilo

INTRO *Soft ballad* (♩ = ca. 108)

VERSES

1. Life can be___ so good,___ life can be___ so hard,
2. Noth - ing is___ for sure, noth - ing is___ for keeps.___

1. nev - er know - ing what___ each day will bring___ to where___ you are.___
2. All I know___ is that___ your love will live___ e - ter - nal - ly. So

1. Some - times I___ for - get,___ and some - times I can't see___
2. I will find___ my rest___ and I will find my peace,___

1. that what - ev - er comes my way,___ you'll be with me.
2. know - ing that___ you'll meet my ev - 'ry need.___ My

REFRAIN

life is in___ your hands,___ my heart is in___ your keep - ing. I'm

nev - er with - out___ hope,___ not when my fu - ture is___ with you.

385

192 Mountain of God

Marc Cavallero, Dan Brennan
and Ken Canedo

Based on Psalm 121

INTRO *With a steady rock beat (= 104-108)*

REFRAIN

I see___ the moun-tain of God, ___ the God who lis-tens to me. ___ Come to___

Mountain of God, ___ lis-tens to me; ___

the moun-tain of God. ___ God will set us all free. ___

moun-tain of God, ___ set us all free. ___

VERSES

1. Where can I turn, O God,___ when I am lost and trou - bled?___
2. Some-times I let you down,___ but you will nev - er fail___ me.
3. You give me hope, O God,___ when I am down and wea - ry.___

1. Give me the faith to see___ that you'll be there for me. Oh,
2. Though I may run and hide,___ you're al - ways at my side. Oh,
3. I can de - pend on you___ to al - ways see me through. Oh,

Nothing Is Beyond You

193

Rich Mullins, Tom Booth and Mitch McVicker

Prayer & Praise Songs

Prayer & Praise Songs

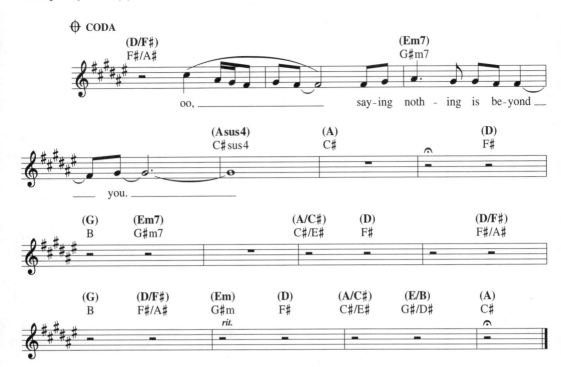

oo, _____ say-ing noth - ing is be-yond ___ you. _____

Now

194

Rory Cooney

REFRAIN *a cappella*

Now is the mo - ment, ___ now is the time. ___

This ver - y day ___ there is sal - va - tion. ___

Melody

Now is the mo - ment, ___ now is the time. ___

Harmony

This ver - y day ___ there is sal - va - tion. ___ *Fine*

VERSES

1a. Don't want a heav - en ___ af - ter I'm gone: ___
1b. Don't want a vi - sion ___ of saints robed in white. ___
2a. Don't want a fu - ture ___ where God sets things right: ___
2b. Don't want a ban - quet ___ in heav - en a - bove ___ 'til
3a. Don't want a king - dom, ___ don't want a crown, ___ 'til
3b. No Ar - ma - ged - don, ___ no thou - sand years, ___

1 **2** **D.S.**

1a. I need a place ___ to keep my fam - i - ly warm.
1b. I want the blind ___ to see the sweet morn - ing light.
2a. I need a neigh - bor - hood to walk safe at night.
2b. no one is hun - gry in this world that I love.
3a. all na - tions lay ___ their an - gry wea - pons down.
3b. no more to - mor - rows! On - ly now. On - ly here.

Prayer & Praise Songs

195 On Eagle's Wings

Michael Joncas
Arranged by Craig Kingsbury

Based on Psalm 91

1. You who dwell in the shel-ter of the Lord, who a-bide in his shad-ow for
3. You need not fear the ter-ror of the night, nor the ar-row that flies by

1. life, say to the Lord: "My ref-uge, my rock in whom I trust!"
3. day; though thou-sands fall a-bout you, near you it shall not come.

REFRAIN

And he will raise you up on ea-gle's wings, bear you on the

breath of dawn, make you to shine like the sun, and

hold you in the palm of his hand.
palm of his hand.

VERSE 2

2. The snare of the fowl-er will nev-er cap-ture you, and
2. fam-ine will bring you no fear: un-der his wings your
2. ref-uge, his faith-ful-ness _____ your shield.

VERSE 4

4. For to his an-gels he's giv-en a com-mand to
4. guard you in all of your ways; up-on their hands they will
4. bear you up, lest you dash your foot a-gainst a stone.

CODA

And hold you, hold you in the
palm _____ of his hand. _____

393

196
Open My Eyes

Based on Mark 8:22–25

Jesse Manibusan

BRIDGE

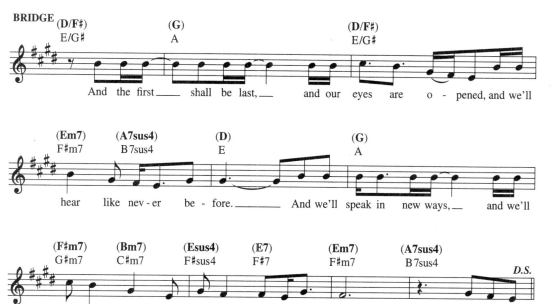

And the first ___ shall be last, ___ and our eyes are o - pened, and we'll

hear like nev - er be - fore. ___ And we'll speak in new ways, ___ and we'll

see God's face in plac - es we've nev - er known.   3. O - pen my

VERSE 4

I live within you. Deep in your heart, O Love.
I live within you. Rest now in me.

197 Our God Reigns

Leonard E. Smith, Jr.
Arranged by Rick Modlin

Isaiah 52:7

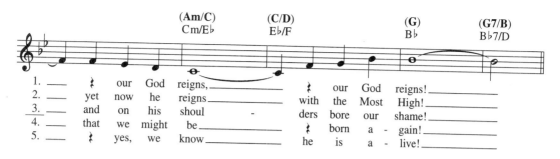

1. ___ ? our God reigns,_____ ? our God reigns!_____
2. ___ yet now he reigns_____ with the Most High!_____
3. ___ and on his shoul - ders bore our shame!_____
4. ___ that we might be_____ ? born a - gain!_____
5. ___ ? yes, we know_____ he is a - live!_____

REFRAIN

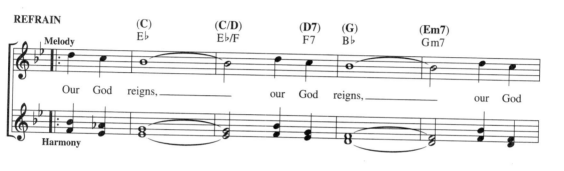

Melody: Our God reigns,_____ our God reigns,_____ our God
Harmony

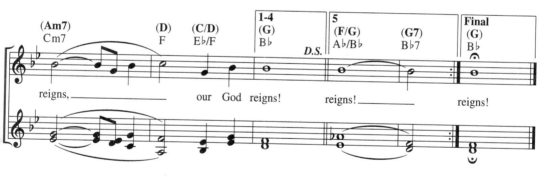

reigns,_____ our God reigns! reigns!_____ reigns!

198 Prayer of Abandonment

Based on a prayer by Br. Charles de Foucauld

Tom Booth

VERSE 3

3. Fa-ther, I sur - ren-der; I ___ place my-self in your hands

3. be - cause you are my fa - ther _____ and be-cause I

3. love you; ___ in - to your ___ hands I com-mend my spir-it. ___

199

Prayer of St. Francis/
Oración de San Francisco

Sebastian Temple

INTRO

VERSES/ESTROFAS 1, 2, 4

1. Make me a chan-nel of your
2. Make me a chan-nel of your
4. Make me a chan-nel of your

1. *Haz-me un ins - tru - men - to de tu*
2. *Haz-me un ins - tru - men - to de tu*
4. *Haz-me un ins - tru - men - to de tu*

1. peace. ___ Where there is ha - tred, let me bring your
2. peace. ___ Where there's de - spair in life, let me bring
4. peace. ___ It is in par - don - ing that we are

1. *paz,* ___ *don - de ha - ya o - dio lle - ve yo tu a -*
2. *paz,* ___ *que lle - ve tu es - pe - ran - za por do -*
4. *paz,* ___ *es per - do - nan - do que nos das per -*

1. love. ___ Where there is in - ju - ry, your par - don, Lord, ___
2. hope. ___ Where there is dark - ness ___ on - ly light, ___
4. par - doned, ___ In giv - ing of our - selves that we re - ceive, ___

1. *mor,* ___ *don - de ha - ya in - ju - ria, tu per - dón, Se - ñor,* ___
2. *quier,* ___ *don - de ha - ya os - cu - ri - dad lle - ve tu luz,* ___
4. *dón,* ___ *es dan - do a to - dos que Tú nos das,* ___

1

1. ___ And ___ where there's doubt, true faith in you. ___
2. ___ And ___ where there's sad - ness
4. ___ And in ___ dy - ing that we're

1. ___ *don - de ha - ya du - da fe en ti.* ___
2. ___ *don - de ha - ya pe - na*
4. ___ *y mu - rien - do es que vol -*

D.S.

2 G7   C   *to Verse 3* || **Final** G7   C   *Fine*

2. ev - er ___ joy. ___   4. born to e - ter - nal life. ___
2. tu go - zo, Se - ñor. ___   4. -ve - mos a na - cer. ___

VERSE/ESTROFA 3

F   C   Am   Dm

3. O Mas - ter, grant that I may nev - er seek ___ So much to be con -
3. Ma - es - tro, a - yú - da - me a nun - ca bus - car ___ el ser ___ con - so -

G7   C   G7   C7   F

3. soled, as to con - sole, ___ To be un - der - stood, as to un - der -
3. la - do si - no con - so - lar, ___ ser en - ten - di - do si - no en - ten -

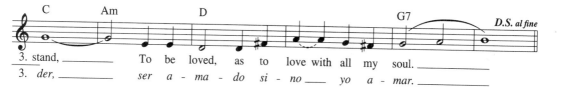

C   Am   D   G7   *D.S. al fine*

3. stand, ___ To be loved, as to love with all my soul. ___
3. der, ___ ser a - ma - do si - no ___ yo a - mar. ___

200

Revive Us, O God

Jesse Manibusan

VERSE 2

1. - ror, can hearts be trans-formed?__ Long-ing for you__ to draw__ near,
1. __ be - fore we cry out__ you al - read - y hear.__ And re -

2. Weak - ened by judg - ment, where is our strength?__ Con -
2. fined by con - fu - sion, our spir - its are spent.__ But this
2. sick - ness no long - er can hide;__ when we
2. choose your way,__ choose your truth,__ when we choose life,__ you re -

201 Seek First

Based on Matthew 6:33

Amy Grant and Wes King

VERSE

They say we need mon - ey___ and pow - er; they say there's no

God up___ a - bove. Don't they know our friend in___ high

plac - es? Noth - ing can be strong - er___ than love.

202 Shine, Jesus, Shine

Graham Kendrick
Arranged by Rick Modlin

Shine, Je-sus, shine;___ fill this land with the Fa-ther's glo-ry.

Blaze, Spir-it, blaze;___ set our hearts on fire.___

Flow, riv-er, flow;___ flood the na-tions with grace and mer-cy.

Send forth your Word,___ Lord, and let there be light.

light.   light.

VERSES

1. Lord, the light of your love is shin - ing, in the midst of the
2. Lord, I come to your awe - some pres - ence, from the shad - ows in -
3. As we gaze on your king - ly bright - ness, so our fac - es dis -

1. dark - ness, shin - ing. Je - sus, Light of the world, shine up -
2. to your ra - diance. By the blood I may en - ter your
3. play your like - ness, ev - er chang - ing from glo - ry to

1. on___ us. Set us free by the truth you now bring___ us.
2. bright - ness. Search me, try me, con - sume all my dark - ness.
3. glo - ry. Mir - rored here, may our lives tell your sto - ry.

1-3. Shine on___ me, shine on___ me.___

203 Sometimes by Step

Rich Mullins and Beaker

INTRO Steady four (♩ = ca. 100)

VERSES

1. Some-times the night___ is beau-ti-ful.
2. Some-times I think___ of A-bra-ham, how

1. Some-times the sky_____ was so___ far a-way.
2. one star he saw___ had been lit___ for him.

Some-times it seems___ to be
He was a strang-er in

1. ___ so close_____ you could touch___ it, but your heart would break.___
2. ___ this land._____ And I am___ that, no___ less than he,___

Some-times the morn-
and on the road__

1. -ing came___ too soon._____ Some-times the day___ could be___ so hard.___
2. ___ to righ-teous-ness._____ Some-times the climb___ can be___ so steep___

1. There was so much___ work left___ to do,___ but so much you'd al-read-y done.
2. I may fal-ter in___ my steps,___ and nev-er be-yond___ your reach.

REFRAIN
Melody

O God, you are my___ God, and I will ev-er praise__ you.

Harmony

204 Strength for the Journey

Michael John Poirier

This Little Light of Mine

205

Traditional

Spiritual

1. This lit - tle light of mine, ___ I'm gon-na let it shine. ___
2. Ev - 'ry - where I go, ___ I'm gon-na let it shine. ___
3. Je - sus gave it to me; ___ I'm gon-na let it shine. ___

1. This lit - tle light of mine, ___ I'm gon-na let it shine. ___
2. Ev - 'ry - where I go, ___ I'm gon-na let it shine. ___
3. Je - sus gave it to me; ___ I'm gon-na let it shine. ___

1. This lit - tle light of mine, ___ I'm gon - na let it shine. _
2. Ev - 'ry - where I go, ___
3. Je - sus gave it to me; ___

1-3. ___ Let it shine, ___ let it shine, ___ let it shine. _

1-2

Final

1-2. _____

3. _____

206 The Call

Tom Franzak

*Verse 1 may begin *a cappella*; chords between brackets are optional.

VERSE 2

CODA

207 The Will of Your Love
(Tu Voluntad)

Text suggested by Brother Roger, Taizé Community
Spanish translation by Pia Moriarty and Bob Hurd

Suzanne Toolan, RSM

OSTINATO REFRAIN/ESTRIBILLO (♩ = ca. 94)

The will of your love, the will of your
Tu vo-lun-tad, tu com-pa-

VERSES/ESTROFAS

1. Bless - ed are you, bless - ed and
1. E - res ben - di - to, tú e - res

2. O - pen my eyes that I may know your
2. Á - bre-me los o - jos a tus ma - ra -

3. O God, teach me
3. Mués - tra - me tu sa - bi - du -

4. A lamp to my feet, a light to my
4. Pa - la - bra de Dios es luz pa - ra mi

5. Hap - py are you who fol - low the path of your
5. Fe - li - ces los que si - guen las sen - das de a -

6. Hap - py are you who walk in
6. Fe - li - ces los que ca - mi - nan en

love be done ___ on ___ earth _____ as it is in heav - en.
- sión ⁊ se - a en la tie - rra co - mo‿en el cie - lo.

1. ho - ly. Teach me your way, the way of your love.
1. san - to. Tus sen - das son ca - mi - nos de‿a - mor.

2. won - ders, the won-ders of your way, the won-ders of your love.
2. - vi - llas, las o - bras de tu‿a - mor que‿en - se - ñan com - pa - sión.

3. wis - dom; O _____ God, the wis-dom of your love.
3. - rí - a. Mués - tra - me ser sa - bio en tu‿a - mor.

4. path _____ is your ___ word, your word _____ of truth.
4. sen - da, es la ver - dad que guí - a mis pies.

5. God, who live in God's love _____ as it is in heav-en.
5. - mor a - quí en la tie - rra co - mo‿en el cie - lo.

6. truth; in you there is no dark-ness, in you ___ there is light.
6. luz, la luz de tu ver - dad. ___ No hay os - cu - ri - dad.

208 There Is a Longing

Anne Quigley

There is a long-ing in our hearts, O Lord, for you to re-
veal your - self to us. ___ There is a long-ing in our
hearts for love we on - ly find in you, our God.

VERSES: *Stronger*

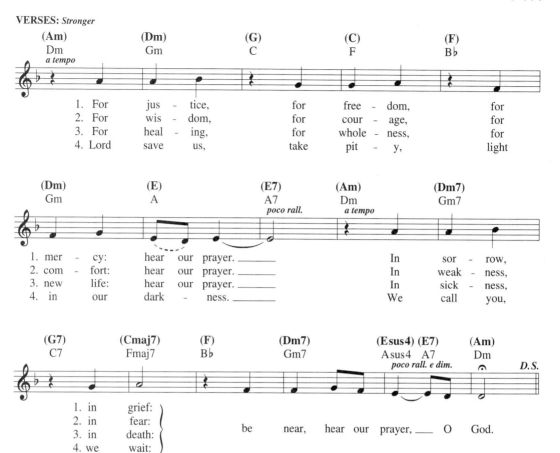

1. For jus - tice, for free - dom, for mer - cy: hear our prayer. In sor - row, in grief:
2. For wis - dom, for cour - age, for com - fort: hear our prayer. In weak - ness, in fear:
3. For heal - ing, for whole - ness, for new life: hear our prayer. In sick - ness, in death:
4. Lord save us, take pit - y, light in our dark - ness. We call you, we wait:

be near, hear our prayer, ___ O God.

209   There Is a Well/Un Pozo Hay

Spanish translation by Jaime Cortez

Tom Conry

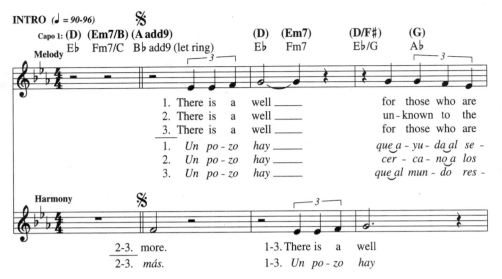

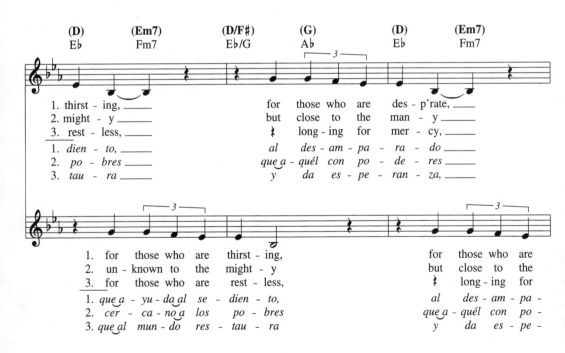

Through It All

Andraé Crouch
Arranged by Peter Quint

INTRO (♩ = ca. 70)

Capo 1: (A) (A7) (D) (D7/F#) (G6) (G/A)
Bb Bb7 Eb Eb7/G Ab6 Ab/Bb

mf

(Keybd)

%. **VERSES**

(D) (Dmaj7)
Eb Ebmaj7

mp

1. I've had man - y tears ___ and sor - rows; I've had ques - tions for ___
2. I've ___ been to lots ___ of plac - es, and I've seen a lot ___
3. I ___ thank God for ___ the moun - tains, and I thank him for ___

(D7)
Eb7

1. ___ to - mor - row; there have been times I did - n't know ___ right from
2. ___ of fac - es; there have been times I felt ___ so ___ all a -
3. ___ the val - leys; I thank him for the storms ___ he ___ brought me

(G) (G/F#) (G/E) (G/D) (C9)
Ab Ab/G Ab/F Ab/Eb Db9

1. wrong; ___ but in ev - 'ry ___ sit - u -
2. lone; ___ but ___ in my ___ lone - ly
3. through; ___ for ___ if I'd ___ nev - er

(D) (B7)
Eb C7

1. a - tion God gave ___ bless - ed ___ con - so - la - tion, that my ___
2. hours, ___ yes, those ___ pre - cious ___ lone - ly hours, ___ Je - sus ___
3. had a prob - lem, I would - n't ___ know that he could solve them, I'd

(Em7) (A7) (D) (Em7) (A7)
Fm7 Bb7 Eb Fm7 Bb7

1. tri - als come ___ to on - ly ___ make me strong.
2. let me know ___ that I ___ was his own.
3. nev - er know ___ what faith in ___ God could do.

REFRAIN

Prayer & Praise Songs

211 Thy Word Is a Lamp

Based on Psalm 119:105
Amy Grant

Michael W. Smith

VERSE 3

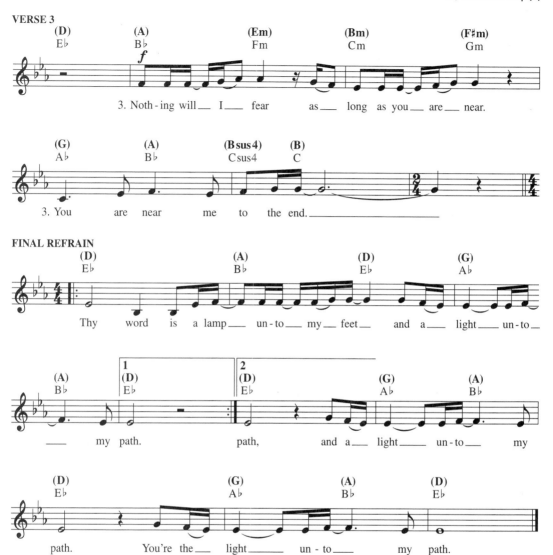

FINAL REFRAIN

212 With All I Am

Mike Nelson

Mike Nelson and Michael Anthony Perna

Lyrics:

REFRAIN

With all I am I come with hum-ble heart, I come with soul re-joic-ing to do your will. With all I am, all I can be, all I of-fer I of-fer for you. you. you.

VERSE 1

1. Teach me your ways, O Lord, and send me forth with your word on my lips and in my heart.

VERSE 2

C♯m7   D   A   F♯m7

2. Let your com - pas - sion live with - in me, so that

F   C   C *(let ring)*   Bm   C♯m   D   D/E   *D.S.*

2. I may give to all as you give to me. _____

VERSE 3

F♯m   G   F♯m   D

3. In all cre - a - tion ___ is your pres - ence. Help me to

A   C *(let ring)*   Bm   C♯m   D   D/E   *D.S.*

3. see you in all I serve. _____

213
You Are the Way

Steve Angrisano, Tom Tomaszek and Christi Smith

Steve Angrisano and Pat Smith

INTRO (♩ = ca. 112)

REFRAIN

You are the Way, you are the Truth, you are the Life, my sal-va-tion. You are the Way, you are the Truth, you are the Life, the gate-way to my soul.

- way to my soul. - way to my soul. You are the Life, the gate - way to my soul.

VERSES 1, 2

1. We __ come to - geth - er now, we cel - e - brate __ and shout,
2. In a world that's mov - ing fast, we seek what will __ not last.

1. for you have shown the way. ___
2. We miss the nar - row road. ___ But

1. ⁊ We lift our voic - es high, we sing, we dance, __ we cry:
2. when we look in - side __ our - selves, we find that no __ one else

1. "You are the on - ly way!" ___
2. but you can make us whole. ___

VERSE 3

3. If we ask you we will __ re - ceive. ___ If we

3. seek you then we __ shall find. Knock, and gates will be o -

3. - pened wide, __ for a might - y God __ has done great things __ for you!

Copyright Acknowledgments

COPYRIGHT HOLDERS AND ADMINISTRATORS

Angelus Records
Toe Jam Music
11435 Essex Ave.
Chino, CA 91710

BMG Songs, Inc. (ASCAP)
Careers-BMG Music Publishing, Inc. (BMI)
Floating Note Music
Kid Brothers of St. Frank Publishing (ASCAP)
1400 - 18th Ave. South
Nashville, TN 37212
615/858-1300

Center for Ministry Development
P.O. Box 699
Naugatuck, CT 06770

Confraternity of Christian Doctrine (CCD)
3211 Fourth St. NE
Washington, DC 20017

THE COPYRIGHT COMPANY
Maranatha! Music
Maranatha Praise, Inc.
40 Music Square East
Nashville, TN 37203

Melanie Croskey, estate of **Steve Croskey**
Tempe, AZ 85283

EMI Christian Music Group
Andi Beat Goes On Music
Ariose Music (ASCAP)
Birdwing Music (ASCAP)
BMG Songs (ASCAP)
Cherry Lane Music Publishing Co., Inc.
Curious? Music U.K. (PRS)
Meadowgreen Music Co.
Mountain Spring Music (ASCAP)
Sparrow Song (BMI)
Straightway Music (ASCAP)
P.O. Box 5084
101 Winner's Circle
Brentwood, TN 37024-5084

G.I.A. Publications, Inc.
7404 S. Mason Ave.
Chicago, IL 60638

Harold Ober Associates, Inc.
425 Madison Ave.
New York, NY 10017

Heartbeat Music
August Music
P.O. Box 20
Donnellson, IA 52625

Hope Publishing Co.
Stainer & Bell Ltd.
380 S. Main Pl.
Carol Stream, IL 60188
630/665-3200
Fax 630/665-2552

Integrity Music, Inc.
Hosanna! Music
Make Way Music
P.O. Box 851622
Mobile, AL 36695-1622

International Commission on English in the Liturgy (ICEL), Inc.
1522 K Street, N.W., Suite 1000
Washington, DC 20005-1202
202/347-0800
Fax 202/347-1839

Lorenz Publishing Co.
P.O. Box 802
Dayton, OH 45401
800/444-1144

The Loving Company
Age to Age Music, Inc. (ASCAP)
Locally Owned Music, Inc. (BMI)
7051 Highway 70 South-No. 188
Nashville, TN 37221

Manna Music, Inc.
P.O. Box 218
Pacific City, OR 97135

Music Services, Inc.
Mercy/Vineyard Publishing
209 Chapelwood Drive
Franklin, TN 37069

New Jerusalem Music
Box 225
Clarksboro, NJ 08020

Oregon Catholic Press
North American Liturgy Resources (NALR)
New Dawn Music, Inc.
TEAM Publications
5536 NE Hassalo
Portland, OR 97213-3638
800/548-8749
Fax 503/282-3486

Oxford University Press
70 Baker Street
London W1M 1DJ
ENGLAND

Michael John Poirier
c/o 1221 E Osborn Rd.
Phoenix, AZ 85014

Resource Publications, Inc.
160 E. Virginia St. - No. 290
San Jose, CA 95112

SOBICAIN
Protasio Gomez
15 Madrid, 28027
SPAIN

Vernacular Hymns Publishing Co.

Walton Music Corporation
Utryck (Sweden)
170 NE 33rd St.
Ft. Lauderdale, FL 33334

Warner Brothers Publications
Interior Music
10585 Santa Monica Blvd.
Los Angeles, CA 90025

White Plastic Bag Music (SESAC)
2911 A West Linden Avenue
Nashville, TN 37212

Word Music, Inc. (ASCAP)
Liturgy Legacy Music
Opryland Music
65 Music Square West,
Nashville, TN 37203

Index of Text and Music Sources

Scriptural Index

Topical/Ritual Index

435

Index of Service Music and Prayers

SERVICE MUSIC FOR MASS

INTRODUCTORY RITES

ENTRANCE SONG (GATHERING OR PROCESSIONAL)
(See Topical and Scriptural Indexes for Appropriate Songs)

RITE OF BLESSING AND SPRINKLING HOLY WATER
1 Come to the River
135 River of Glory
41 Streams of Living Water

PENITENTIAL RITE
33 Kyrie (Manibusan)
42 Kyrie (Roscoe)
3 Kyrie Eleison (Hurd)
2 Lord, Have Mercy

GLORIA
20 Glory to God (Angrisano/Tomaszek)
27 Glory to God (Booth)
4 Glory to God (Canedo/Hurd)
43 Glory to God (Ho Lung)
34 Glory to God Most High (Manibusan)

LITURGY OF THE WORD

ALLELUIA
44 Advent/Christmas Gospel Acclamation
21 Alleluia (Angrisano/Tomaszek)
28 Alleluia (Booth)
35 Alleluia (Manibusan)
5 Alleluia! Give the Glory (Canedo)
45 Celtic Alleluia
130 Nadie en el Sepulcro/No One in the Tomb

LENTEN GOSPEL ACCLAMATION
46 Glory and Praise
6 Praise and Honor

PROFESSION OF FAITH
29 Profession of Faith

GENERAL INTERCESSIONS
7 General Intercessions (Canedo/Hurd)
8 General Intercessions (Hurd)
48 Hear Our Prayer
36 Tuhan Dengar Doa Kami

LITURGY OF THE EUCHARIST

PREPARATION OF THE ALTAR AND THE GIFTS
(See Topical and Scriptural Indexes for Appropriate Songs)

EUCHARISTIC PRAYER

PREFACE DIALOGUE
9 Introductory Dialogue

HOLY
22 Holy (Angrisano/Tomaszek)
30 Holy (Booth)
10 Holy (Canedo/ Hurd)
37 'Oku, 'Oku Ma'oni'oni

MEMORIAL ACCLAMATION A
23 Christ Has Died
38 Cristo Ha Muerto
31 Memorial Acclamation A (Booth)
11 Memorial Acclamation A (Canedo/Hurd)

MEMORIAL ACCLAMATION B
24 Dying You Destroyed Our Death
12 Memorial Acclamation B

MEMORIAL ACCLAMATION C
13 Memorial Acclamation C

MEMORIAL ACCLAMATION D
14 Memorial Acclamation D

DOXOLOGY AND AMEN
15 Doxology and Great Amen (Canedo/Hurd)
16 Doxology and Great Amen (Canedo/Hurd)

AMEN
25 Amen (Angrisano/Tomaszek)
32 Amen (Booth)
39 Cantamos Amen (Manibusan)

COMMUNION RITE

LORD'S PRAYER
17 Lord's Prayer
49 Our Father

BREAKING OF THE BREAD
40 Lay Chiên Thiên Chúa
26 Lamb of God (Angrisano)
50 Lamb of God (Fisher)
19 Lamb of God (Hurd)
18 Lamb of God (Hurd)

COMMUNION SONG
(See Topical and Scriptural Indexes for Appropriate Songs)

PERIOD OF SILENCE OR SONG OF PRAISE
(See Topical and Scriptural Indexes for Appropriate Songs)

CONCLUDING RITE

CLOSING SONG (SENDING FORTH OR RECESSIONAL)
(See Topical and Scriptural Indexes for Appropriate Songs)

THE LITURGY OF THE HOURS

MORNING PRAYER

INVITATORY PSALM
73 Come, Worship the Lord

MORNING PSALMS, CANTICLES, HYMNS
118 I Am the Light of the World
127 Lord of All Hopefulness
120 Morning Has Broken
68 My Soul Is Thirsting/As Morning Breaks
134 Rain Down
65 Shouts of Joy
62 Taste and See

GOSPEL CANTICLE
94 Canticle of Zachary
93 Canticle of Zechariah

EVENING PRAYER

THANKSGIVING FOR THE LIGHT
52 There Is a Light

EVENING PSALMS, CANTICLES, HYMNS
87 God's Love Is Everlasting
152 Here I Am, Lord
117 How Can I Keep from Singing
118 I Am the Light of the World
84 I Rejoiced
187 Jesus Christ, Inner Light
90 Let My Prayer Come like Incense
127 Lord of All Hopefulness
88 Lord, Your Love Is Everlasting
85 Qué Alegría/I Rejoiced
51 Radiant Light Divine
134 Rain Down
203 Sometimes by Step
61 The Lord Is My Light
211 Thy Word Is a Lamp

GOSPEL CANTICLE
95 Holy Is His Name
96 Holy Is Your Name

NIGHT PRAYER

NIGHT PSALMS AND HYMNS
127 Lord of All Hopefulness
195 On Eagle's Wings
196 Open My Eyes
203 Sometimes by Step

PRAYERS FOR COMMON OCCASIONS

438

Index of First Lines and Common Titles